The Forgotten Silicon Valley

John Howells

Tangible press

The Forgotten Silicon Valley

Tangible Press is a wholly owned and operated subdivision of Punk Hart Productions LLC

Cover design by John Howells

Printed in the United States of America
First Printing, 2020

ISBN: 1-7334579-7-6
ISBN-13: 978-1-7334579-7-2

Library of Congress Control Number: 2020922199

“Computers are like Old Testament gods; lots of rules and no mercy.”

— *Joseph Campbell, The Power of Myth*

“That's the thing about people who think they hate computers. What they really hate is lousy programmers.”

— *Larry Niven*

“I really didn't foresee the Internet. But then, neither did the computer industry. Not that that tells us very much of course – the computer industry didn't even foresee that the century was going to end.”

— *Douglas Adams*

“‘All of a sudden, we’ve lost a lot of control,’ he said. ‘We can’t turn off our internet; we can’t turn off our smartphones; we can’t turn off our computers. You used to ask a smart person a question. Now, who do you ask? It starts with g-o, and it’s not God…’”

— *Steve Wozniak*

Table of Contents

Introduction

Everybody knows the story. In the late 1960s and early 1970s some entrepreneurs living in the Santa Clara Valley in northern California started up some small computer shops in their garages and set the world on fire, leading to the technology that we're all familiar with in the present day and leading to the designation of Silicon Valley. But there's more to the story. Apple, Hewlett-Packard, Intel and others were the dominant computer software and hardware companies in the valley, but this is not about them. This story is about the "forgotten" Silicon Valley and the way it was in the early days, before the world discovered the Internet and the fun and convenience of the hand-held devices upon which modern day society revolves. This is also a personal story of what it was like growing up in Silicon Valley, before it was known as such, and how easy it was to become involved in the technological revolution that was at the center of the valley. The real story I am about to unfold may amaze you.

I first came to the Santa Clara Valley in 1958 as a child and lived in San Jose, California. Prior to that, my early years were spent on the road, living in a large travel trailer, going from town to town throughout the United States where my parents both worked as "tramp printers,"[1] an occupation which allowed a member of the Typographical Union to work at any newspaper in the country once you presented your union card, and of course assuming there was an open position or two. I landed in San Jose for a number of reasons, including the fact that I was old enough to start school and San Jose looked like a very nice place to settle. Indeed, it was. At the time, San Jose was known for its central role in the valley for its magnificent orchards and farms, the main crops being apricots and prunes. Any technological inventions bubbling beneath the surface were still a long way away, but in the late 1950s and early 1960s you could hardly think of a better place to grow up or to raise your family.

The term Silicon Valley refers to the silicon-based semiconductors made possible by Nobel Prize winner William

---

[1] See the book *Tramp Printers* written by my father and his co-author Marion Dearman for a look into that fascinating lifestyle.

Shockley (known as the father of the transistor) of Bell Labs in Palo Alto. Hewlett-Packard was also started in Palo Alto, so that city (where Stanford University resides) is essentially the birthplace of the technological advances that the valley has become famous for, but in reality it was not until the mid 1990s that the world at large became aware of the work being done by the scientists and nerdy teenagers living in the areas surrounding Palo Alto. Other important cities in Santa Clara County were Sunnyvale, Cupertino, Mountain View, and eventually San Jose and Los Gatos.

Over time, the agricultural importance of the Santa Clara Valley became diminished as the rise of personal computing exploded in the late '90s – usually referred to as the Dot-Com boom. There will be more about that later in Chapter Nine ("Startup Fever"), but for now here is a partial list of the Silicon Valley companies that continue to be known and continue to dominate the industry: Apple (Cupertino), Hewlett-Packard (Palo Alto), Oracle (Redwood Shores), Adobe (San Jose), Netflix (Los Gatos), Google (Mountain View), Facebook (Menlo Park), to name just a few. But there is a whole slew of once giant companies that fell from grace and are barely remembered today, even though at one time they were seen as unstoppable giants. Later in this book I will discuss the most important "missing" companies, but the story I want to tell begins now.

Chapter 1: The Valley of Heart's Delight

Why "Silicon Valley"? How did this term originate? As it turns out, we know exactly where and when it was first coined, but we'll get to that later. For the moment, let us look at the early days of the Santa Clara Valley, which as we probably all know, is a region in Northern California not too far from San Francisco, and is widely known as the tech capitol of the world. How did that happen, and why was the Santa Clara Valley the ideal location for most modern technological advances to occur? To understand this, we need to look at what the valley used to be before it became what it is today.

At the beginning of the 20th century, if the region was known for anything at all, it was known for its agriculture and its superior farmland and fine orchards. Some of the crops grown in the valley included prunes, apricots, as well as carrots, almonds, walnuts, pears and cherries. In fact, until the 1960s it was the largest fruit producing and packing region in the world. For a time it was known as "The Valley of Heart's Delight", although it is not completely certain where that term came from and whether or not it obtained popularity, but at the very least it is the title of a Chamber of Commerce film designed to promote the area for business interests, as well as drawing families to settle in the valley. Regardless, the region was indeed ideal for growing crops, as well as raising cattle, and was an ideal location for settling down and raising a family. It was the central region in the state of California for all sorts of things, and its location allowed for easy access to San Francisco and the Pacific Ocean. One of the selling points was the year-round mild weather, which allowed for increased farming and harvesting.

San Jose – Heart of the Valley

Even though San Jose was not the initial location where the computer industry got its start in the valley, it's of special interest to note that the city of San Jose, in the heart of the valley, was the first town in California, having been founded in 1777 by the Franciscan monks, and at one time it was the state capitol. Also, what may come as a surprise is that San Jose had the world's very first radio station with regularly scheduled programming. Established in 1909 by Charles "Doc" Herrold, it broadcast music, news and advertisements. The station lives on today in San Francisco as KCBS.

For many reasons San Jose, and the outlying cities in the valley – such as Cupertino, Mountain View and Sunnyvale – all play a major role in the tech industries that thrive in the region now commonly referred to as Silicon Valley. But there is something very special about San Jose that makes it worthy of further examination.

San Jose is famous for its biggest tourist attraction: The Winchester Mystery House. You've probably heard of this, especially if you happened to see the 2018 film *Winchester*, which turns the life of Sarah Winchester, heir to the

Winchester Rifle fortune, into a ghost story. Sarah Winchester moved from New Haven, Connecticut, to San Jose in 1886. She is one of the most famous residents of what would eventually become Silicon Valley.

MRS. SARAH WINCHESTER
ONLY KNOWN PORTRAIT IN EXISTENCE

The legend surrounding her is that she was heavily into spiritualism and believed that she was cursed by the souls of those killed by the Winchester rifle, and the only way to alleviate the curse was to keep building onto her San Jose mansion, which she did until her death. The House has many oddities and anomalous features. There are rooms within rooms. There is a staircase that leads nowhere, abruptly halting at the ceiling. In another place, there is a door which opens into a solid wall. Some of the House's 47 chimneys have an overhead ceiling—while, in some places, there are skylights covered by a roof—and some skylights are covered by another skylight—and, in one place, there is a skylight built into the floor. There are tiny doors leading into large spaces, and large doors that lead into very small spaces. In another part of the House, a second story door opens outward to a sheer drop to the ground below. Moreover, upside-down pillars can be found all about the House. All in all, a fascinating house to visit on a guided tour.

San Jose was, and still is, known for a few other tourist attractions. One of them is the Rosicrucian Egyptian Museum & Planetarium, more popularly known as just "the Egyptian Museum", which is located in the Rose Garden neighborhood – itself a big San Jose attraction. The Egyptian Museum has the largest collection of ancient Egyptian artifacts in North America. It was founded by the Ancient Mystical Order Rosae Crucis (AMORC), which itself was founded by Harvey Spencer Lewis, a collector of mystical artifacts from the Far East. The museum was founded in San Jose in 1928 because, not only was it a desirable location not far from San Francisco, it was affordable. One of the most appealing aspects of the Santa Clara Valley in the early part of the 20th century was the cheap real estate, especially compared to San Francisco.

I, myself, visited the Egyptian Museum many times as a child, mostly through school field trips. I remember seeing at least one mummy there. It wasn't until many years later that I learned about the connection to the Rosicrucian society. If you ever pass through San Jose, you owe it to yourself to visit this unique location.

James Lick circa unknown

Then there's the world-famous James Lick Observatory, named after James Lick (another famous San Jose resident), located on top of Mt. Hamilton just east of San Jose. James Lick was once the wealthiest person living in California, due to his real estate investments in the Bay Area, particularly in San Francisco in the early days of the Gold Rush. Among his many accomplishments was the building of what was regarded as the finest hotel in the West – The Lick House in San Francisco. It was destroyed in the great San Francisco earthquake of 1906. He planted orchards in San Jose and built the largest flour mill in the state. Of special interest to me, he also founded the Ghirardelli Chocolate Company. The chocolate factory is still a major tourist attraction in San Francisco.

After suffering a stroke, Lick was looking for a way to

dispose of his vast fortune and was persuaded to donate his money to the establishment of a mountaintop observatory which ultimately became known as James Lick Observatory in the Diablo mountain range near San Jose. He did this with one stipulation: that he would be buried beneath the observatory upon his death, which makes it his tomb as well. The observatory was the world's first permanently occupied mountaintop observatory and among its importance was the discovery of several moons around Jupiter. James Lick died in 1876, but his legacy lives on with James Lick Observatory. Many a time the family and I would take the trip up to visit the observatory, and it was a popular destination for school field trips. During the winter there was plenty of snow there, although it was extremely rare to see any snow in the Santa Clara Valley itself, so it was a nice treat to go up to the summit of Mt. Hamilton to actually be able to play in the snow.

Another famous east side San Jose attraction was Alum Rock Park, located in the valley of the Diablo range on the way up to Mt. Hamilton. It is California's oldest municipal park, established in 1872, and includes 720 acres of hiking trails, picnic grounds, a large public swimming pool (in which I spent many an afternoon in the summer), and a number of campgrounds. I used to ride my bike up there in the summer to use the pool or hike along the trails.

Added to all that, there was Frontier Village. This was a once popular theme park that was intended to duplicate the look and feel of a western town, complete with fake gunfights, saloons, rides, gift shops, and my favorite attraction: authentic stagecoach rides! Frontier Village, which existed from 1961 until 1980, was a popular destination for high school graduation parties when I was going to school.

Frontier Village was located in Edenvale Garden Park, which was once part of the vast Hayes estate, and herein tells the tale of another important inhabitant of the Santa Clara Valley – Everis A. Hayes, a congressman, fruit grower, miner and owner of both the San Jose Mercury and San Jose Herald. Both papers merged into one and today the San Jose Mercury still exists as a major Northern California paper. Incidentally, both my father and mother worked for the Mercury, which is how I wound up being a part of the future Silicon Valley.

Today, even though Frontier Village is gone, done in by urban sprawl and intense competition from Marriot's Great America in Santa Clara, the Hayes Mansion lives on as a landmark of San Jose. One of the companies I worked for hosted a party there, so I got to experience the mansion firsthand.

Another thing that the pre-Silicon Valley San Jose is famous for is its thriving psychedelic garage band music scene. Anyone over the age of 60 (ahem!) will no doubt remember hearing the song "Psychotic Reaction" on the radio. The hit single peaked at #5 on the U.S. charts in 1966 and is still a staple of classic rock radio. The band who recorded this one-hit wonder was San Jose's own Count Five. Likewise, oldsters such as I will surely remember the song "Little Girl" (look it up on YouTube). This one-hit wonder was recorded by San Jose's Syndicate of Sound and the single reached #8 on the U.S. charts in 1966. Then there's the Chocolate Watch Band, formed in Los Altos but long considered to be a San Jose band due to their huge following in that city and the number of shows played there, but they played all over the Bay Area, including the Fillmore Auditorium in San Francisco where promoter Bill Graham expressed an interest in signing them to a management contract. Although they never had any big charting singles, they appeared in the films "Riot on Sunset Strip" and "The Love-Ins" and to this day have a strong cult following as one of the premier garage bands of the 1960s. Again, check YouTube to hear what these bands sound like.

There are a number of other San Jose bands worth mentioning, such as People! (featuring Larry Norman, later to become world famous as one of the pioneers of modern Christian Rock), Teddy and His Patches and Stained Glass, but by far the most famous band to come out of San Jose has to have been the Doobie Brothers. I could write an entire chapter on just this band alone, but I'm sure that won't be necessary. The hit singles "Listen to the Music", "China Grove" and "Black Water," among others, should be enough to give you an idea of how popular they were in the 1970s, and continue to be to this day.

STEREO
People!
I LOVE YOU

STAINED GLASS
CRAZY HORSE ROADS

STEREO
orphan egg
CAROLE

PSYCHOTIC REVELATION
The Ultimate
COUNT FIVE

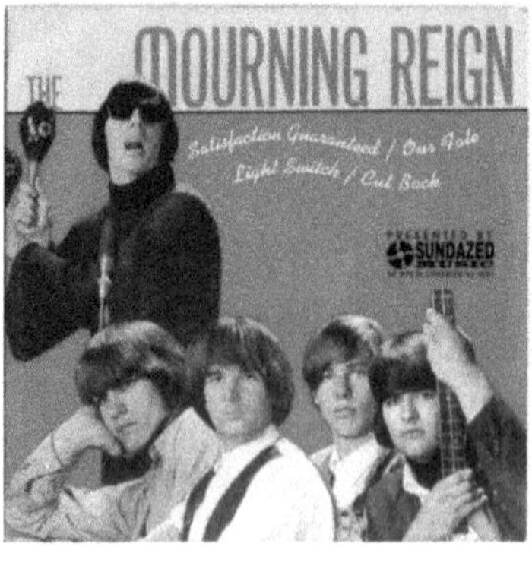
THE MOURNING REIGN
Satisfaction Guaranteed / Our Fate
Light Switch / Cut Back
SUNDAZED

THE DOOBIE BROTHERS

As we can see, the Santa Clara Valley, and San Jose in particular, was one of the best places to live and work in all of California, and indeed in all of the United States; but in order for any sort of technological growth to have occurred, there must have been reasons, other than the mild climate and cheap real estate, why some of the early tech pioneers chose this particular location to start the businesses that would spur such technological marvels that we are all familiar with today. As it turns out, it was a series of accidents and serendipitous choices made by certain individuals that made it all possible. We will focus on three such individuals who, either by design or by chance, brought about the early stages of research and development that made it all possible.

Leland Stanford

Amasa Leland Stanford founded Stanford University in 1885, and to most people this may not seem like a significant event in the history of what is currently known as Silicon Valley, but the importance cannot be understated.

Leland Stanford as he became known, was born in New York in 1824 and moved to California during the Gold Rush in 1852. He started out as a merchant and wholesaler, running a general store for the miners in what was once known as Michigan City but is now known as Michigan Bluff, and became very successful when he moved his business to Sacramento. His rise as a successful businessman led him on a political path which took him to one term as Governor of California – the eighth person to occupy the office – and later a US Senator for eight years. While he was Governor, he oversaw the establishment of California's first state university – San Jose State University, established in 1857 before the Civil War.

Stanford really made a name for himself as a railroad man and is considered to be a "robber baron", mainly due to his reputation for using dishonest methods to increase his wealth. For instance, in 1868 he acquired control of the Southern Pacific Railroad while still serving as Governor and he approved millions of dollars in state grants for the construction of a transcontinental railroad line when he was also president of the Central Pacific Railroad. This was more than a conflict of interest. He also used his considerable assets to bribe congressmen and others with political influence in the country's capital. Furthermore, he extorted local governments into providing millions of dollars in subsidies by threatening to have the rail line bypass their communities. He was also director of Wells Fargo from 1870 to 1884 and started the insurance company Pacific Mutual Life, now known as Pacific Life.

A man of many interests, he also owned two wineries and founded the Palo Alto Stock Farm, where he bred horses. It was due to his interest in racehorses that he participated, accidentally, in the creation of motion pictures. In 1872, Stanford hired photographer Eadweard Muybridge to film horses trotting and galloping so he could determine, as part of a wager, if they had all four feet off the ground at the same time. To accomplish this, he had Muybridge set up a series of cameras that would photograph, in a stop-motion sort of way, one shot per second. When the results were viewed, much as you would view drawings in a flipbook, it was easy to see that not only did the horse indeed have all four feet off the ground at times, but also you could see the horse running in a continuous manner that demonstrated that you could do the same with any other circumstance. Thus, by accident, the development of the motion picture camera was begun.

In 1884, while on a trip to Italy, his teenage son died of typhoid. Completely devastated by this tragedy, Leland Stanford and his wife Jane established Stanford University in 1885 to honor their son, donating approximately $40 million to develop the University, which was intended to model east coast universities such as Harvard and Yale. The University was originally intended to focus on agricultural studies, but of course today we are more familiar with Stanford

Stanford University

University as a medical and law school. The first student enrolled, as it turns out, was future President Herbert Hoover.

Unfortunately, Stanford also had an ugly racist streak, which was not all that unusual for people of power in the 1880s. He had this to say about Chinese immigrants:

> To my mind it is clear, that the settlement among us of an

> inferior race is to be discouraged by every legitimate means. Asia, with her numberless millions, sends to our shores the dregs of her population. Large numbers of this class are already here; and, unless we do something early to check their immigration, the question, which of the two tides of immigration, meeting upon the shores of the Pacific, shall be turned back, will be forced upon our consideration, when far more difficult than now of disposal. There can be no doubt but that the presence among us of numbers of degraded and distinct people must exercise a deleterious influence upon the superior race, and to a certain extent, repel desirable immigration.

Since it was known that Leland Stanford used Chinese workers for his railroad business, he was soon called out as a hypocrite.

Leland Stanford died of heart failure in Palo Alto in 1893. Obviously, he did not live to see the development of the high-tech industries that permeated the Santa Clara Valley one hundred years after his passing, but none of it would have been possible without the existence of Stanford University.

Frederick Terman

The next important development in what was to one day become known as Silicon Valley involved Frederick Terman. Born in 1900 in Indiana, Terman completed his undergraduate degree in chemistry and his master's degree in electrical engineering at Stanford University. He went on to earn his Doctor of Science degree in electrical engineering from MIT in 1924, after which he returned to Stanford University to become a member of the engineering faculty. In this capacity, he designed a study course focusing on work with vacuum tubes, circuits, and instrumentation. With Charles Litton, he established a vacuum tube laboratory at Stanford. This was an extremely important development and soon established Stanford as one of the top schools for electrical engineering, which led to the future of the semi-conductor industry. Among his students at Stanford were William Hewlett and David Packard, who would go on to create one of the most important and longest lasting high-tech companies in the world. Hewlett-Packard products are still being used to this day.

Perhaps the most important development in the region was his encouragement to his students to form their own companies. He personally invested in many of them, resulting in firms such as Litton Industries, Varian Associates, and Hewlett-Packard.

During World War II, Terman directed an organization at Harvard University devoted to research into radar technology, resulting in new technologies that significantly reduced the effectiveness of radar-directed anti-aircraft fire from the enemy. When he was finished with his wartime activities, he returned to Stanford to become Dean of the School of Engineering. In an extremely important development in the region, he led the creation of Stanford Research Park in 1951, and at that time the University leased portions of the park to high-tech firms such as Varian Associates, Hewlett-Packard, Eastman Kodak, General Electric, and Lockheed. Thus, the creation of Silicon Valley was well underway, although the public at large did not realize it at the time. The valley was still primarily an agricultural oasis and not widely recognized for its technological accomplishments.

Terman died in 1982 in Palo Alto. Because of his important achievements, the Terman Middle School and Terman Park were named after him and his father, Lewis Terman, also an important figure in Palo Alto history[2]. However, in 2018 the Palo Alto Unified School District voted unanimously to remove Terman's name from the school due to

---

[2] Ranked as one of the 100 most eminent psychologists of the 20th century.

Lewis Terman's interest in Eugenics. This is a set of theories and practices, widely discredited, whereby proponents aimed to improve the human race by excluding certain races and cultures from breeding, thus (in their minds) improving the genetic makeup of humans[3]. In most people's minds, this was what the Nazis were all about. There is no evidence that son Frederick was a proponent of Eugenics, but he was tarred with the same brush as his father and his honor was perhaps unfairly revoked. Nevertheless, he remains one of the most important figures in the early history of Silicon Valley.

---

[3] For a humorous look at how this might play out, see the movie "Idiocracy", in which mankind continues to favor the dumbest over the more intelligent to the point where 500 years in the future the average person of today would appear to be a genius. On a more serious note, the film "Gattaca" deals with a dystopian society that uses Eugenics to determine what roles specific humans play in society.

William Shockley

The third most significant person in the early development of technology in the valley was William Shockley. Born in London in 1910, he was raised in Palo Alto. He had a distinguished career during World War II where his radar research contributed significantly to the war effort. During this time, he was asked to estimate the number of casualties that might occur in the event of an invasion of Japan. His estimates led to the decision to use the atomic bomb to end the war.

After the war he moved to New Jersey to work at Bell Labs. It was there that he won, along with John Bardeen and Walter Braittain, the 1956 Nobel Prize in Physics for his research on transistors and semi-conductors. Considered to be the inventor of the transistor, although the credit should be shared along with Bardeen and Braittain, Shockley's significance to the history of Silicon Valley cannot be underestimated, but due to a falling out among the three, both Bardeen and Braittain had little to do with subsequent transistor development, which is why Shockley is remembered as the primary inventor of the transistor.

After winning the Nobel Prize in 1956, Shockley moved to Mountain View, California, to start Shockley Semi-conductor Laboratory. Shockley's work served as the basis for many electronic developments for decades, and his company was the first to focus on silicon semiconductor devices in the valley. Over the next forty years, Mountain View would become a primary location for tech companies in the valley.

The reason why silicon is important to the computer industry is because of its chemical makeup. It's neither a metal nor a non-metal but instead is a metalloid – something that is between the two. This makes it the ideal conductor of electricity, and also an insulator, making it the perfect element for creating microchips. It was discovered by Antoine Lavoisier, 18th century French chemist.

But it turns out Shockley was something of a tyrant, or at least was perceived as one by his colleagues. It got to the point where in 1957 eight of them decided to resign and formed their own company in San Jose: Fairchild Semi-conductor – a giant in Silicon Valley to this day. The formation of Fairchild dealt a tremendous blow to Shockley and his company Shockley Semiconductor. Fairchild was now the leader in the semiconductor technology and many new companies emerged from it.

In Shockley's later years, his reputation dimmed quite a bit when, like Lewis Terman and others, he became a proponent of Eugenics. This caused great damage to his reputation and placed him in the public mind in the same category as Adolph Hitler and his Nazi regime. Here's a quote from Shockley:

> My research leads me inescapably to the opinion that the major cause of the American Negro's intellectual and social deficits is hereditary and racially genetic in origin and, thus, not remediable to a major degree by practical improvements in the environment.

Shockley also proposed that individuals with IQs below 100 be paid to undergo voluntary sterilization. By the time of his death in 1989, he had pretty much been ostracized by his friends and family. This was an ignominious end to one of the true giants and founders of Silicon Valley. It also brought into light the heretofore "secret racist history of Silicon Valley."

The Origin of the Name "Silicon Valley"

As indicated at the beginning of this chapter, we know exactly where the name originated. It came from an article called "Silicon Valley USA" written by Don Hoefler. It first appeared in the January 11, 1971 issue of *Electronic News*. In truth, Hoefler didn't invent the name; the story goes that he heard a marketing person use the term at a lunch meeting and he took note and used it in the afore-mentioned article in *Electronic News*. The name didn't gain widespread popularity until the 1980s, when the IBM PC and the Apple II and other emerging home computer systems became prevalent. The Internet (for the consumer market) was still about a decade away, but the name was gradually becoming something the public at large was aware of. For me, I knew the name had reached widespread popularity when I was driving north on Highway 101 in San Jose on my way to work and saw that the exit known as Bernal Road had suddenly had the designation Silicon Valley Boulevard added to it. In truth, there was nothing on that particular stretch of highway that had anything at all to do with high-tech. If you were to take that exit, it would lead you to some strawberry fields instead.

Now the valley I had grown up in since my early childhood was a tourist attraction, in a brand-new way, for people visiting the region on their way to San Francisco.

Typical Santa Clara Valley orchard.

Harvesting crops in San Jose

Typical Pruneyard drying grounds

Downtown San Jose 1920

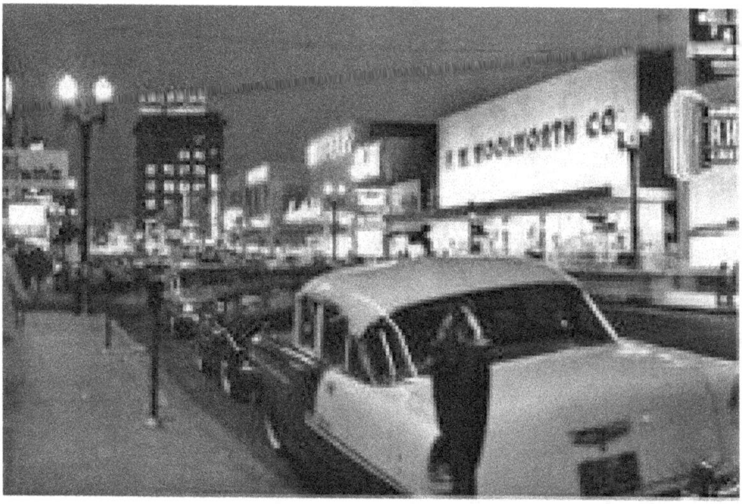

Downtown San Jose in the 1950s

Top and bottom: The Winchester Mystery House in San Jose

The James Lick Observatory

Alum Rock Park in San Jose

Frontier Village in San Jose

The Hayes Mansion in San Jose

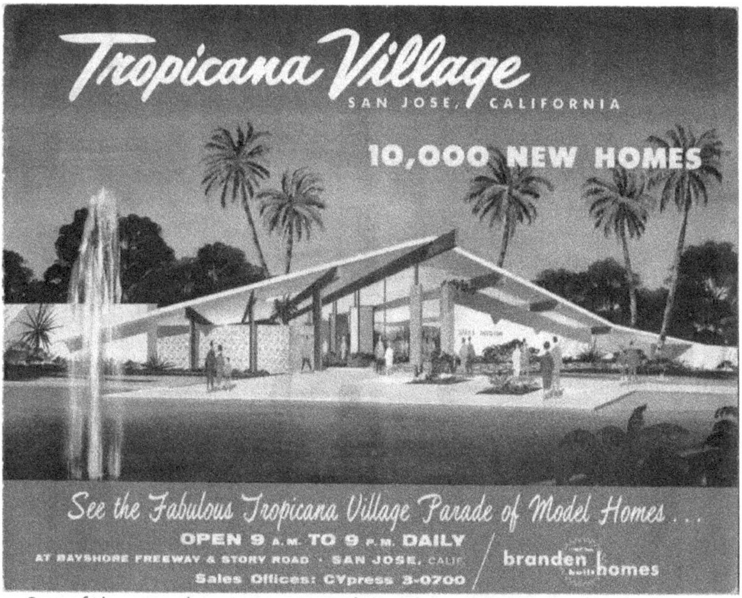

One of the many housing projects that sprang up in San Jose in the late 1950s.

The original Togo's started in San Jose near San Jose State University.

THE PRUNE INDUSTRY. Plate I.

THE CALIFORNIA PRUNE.
(P. d'Agen)

Palo Alto in 1896

University Avenue in Palo Alto, circa 1930

University Avenue, Palo Alto, circa 1950s

Stanford University today

SILICON VALLEY U.S.A.

(This is the first of a three-part series on the history of the semiconductor industry in the Bay Area, a behind-the-scenes report of the men, money, and litigation which spawned 23 companies — from the fledgling rebels of Shockley Transistor to the present day.)

By **DON C. HOEFLER**

It was not a vintage year for semiconductor start-ups. Yet the 1970 year-end box score on the San Francisco Peninsula and Santa Clara Valley of California found four more new entries in the IC sweeps, one more than in 1969.

The pace has been so frantic that even hardened veterans of the semiconductor wars find it hard to realize that the Bay Area story covers an era of only 15 years. And only 23 years have passed since the invention of the transistor, which made it all possible.

For the story really begins on the day before Christmas Eve, Dec. 23, 1947. That was the day, at Bell Telephone Laboratories in Murray Hill, N.J., three distinguished scientists, Dr. John Bardeen, Dr. Walter Brattain and Dr. William Shockley, demonstrated the first successful transistor. It was made of germanium, a point-contact device that looked something like a crystal detector, complete with cat's whiskers.

The three inventors won the Nobel Prize for their efforts, but only one of them, Dr. Shcckley, was determined to capitalize on the transistor commercially. In him lies the genesis of the San Francisco silicon story.

It was only by a quirk of fate, however, coupled with lack of management foresight, that Boston failed to become the major semiconductor center San Francisco is today. When Dr. Shockley left Bell Labs in 1954, he headed first for New England to become a consultant to Raytheon Co., with a view toward establishing a semiconductor firm there under its auspices.

The article that started it all

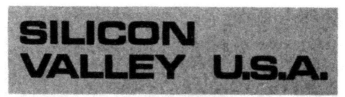

Chapter 2: Can You Start Tonight?

When I moved to the Bay Area in 1958, I was but a child five-years old. It was in the middle of a post-war housing boom that saw the Santa Clara Valley begin to transition into a suburban oasis with close proximity to the city of San Francisco, but rural enough to be the perfect place to raise a family. Where I was raised, it was mostly orchards and ranches. The main crop was prunes, but apricots also played a big part in the area in which I lived. Most kids growing up in the East Foothills picked prunes and/or cut apricots during the summer, earning a few extra dollars to buy toys and candy at the local Woolworths. It was just that simple. Never, for the entire time I was growing up in the South Bay, right up through my teenage years, did I know there was any sort of technological activity in the area. It seemed to me that the major industries in the valley were the canneries and the local Ford plant, not to mention a major newspaper – The San Jose Mercury News, where both of my parents worked. Nothing seemed out of the ordinary. It was just like any other town.

Moffett Field

Hangar One at Moffett Field

I suppose I had driven by Moffett Field many times, but I never knew what went on there. A little bit of information about Moffett Field and its importance to the development of what was to become Silicon Valley: In the 1930s, the US

Military saw that the South Bay, and Santa Clara County in particular, would make a great site strategically to provide a Naval Air base, especially as a place to house their dirigibles. Admiral William A. Moffett was appointed to be the first Chief of the Naval Bureau of Aeronautics, and thus Naval Air Station (NAS) Moffett Field was born. Moffett Field was a significant presence in the Santa Clara Valley, and many businesses sprouted up in the area to support the base. In 1939, NACA (National Advisory Committee for Aeronautics) established Ames Research Center in the base. It was named in honor of Joseph S. Ames, a physicist and one of founding members of NACA.

The emphasis was on Earthly aeronautics, but eventually NACA became NASA (National Aeronautics and Space Administration) because of the burgeoning space race. This is where I come in.

In 1972 I was 19 years old and out of a job. I had been working a pretty good paying job in the mailroom at a local printing plant, thanks to connections through my father who was a printer at the time. The problem with the mailroom job was that it was temporary. I was one of the persons on call in case one of the permanent workers decided to take some time off. They basically "hired a sub", which was what I was. But it was inconsistent, and I was suddenly going for weeks without being called in. There was nothing particularly skilled about the work, so it wasn't because they found someone more skilled; it was just assembly line work, and I never turned down the opportunity to do the job. It was just circumstances that caused me to look for a more permanent position, otherwise I might have spent my entire career working in a mailroom or some other capacity at a number of printing plants.

By chance, a good friend of mine, Doug Merchent, was working at Ames Research Center at Moffett Field as a Computer Operator and they needed someone for the graveyard shift to replace a worker who had suddenly quit. I had never seen a computer in real life before, but I was certainly willing to interview for the job. I had no skills and no college degree. I was more interested in playing in my band and just needed some money to pay the rent and buy food. I could have looked for any number of minimum wage jobs, but since I had the opportunity to pursue this job, I was going to go for it. I already knew that the job only paid minimum wage. It was a government contract job supporting the civil service staff, so money-wise I might as well have been working at McDonalds or Taco Bell. What the hell did I know?

So off I went that afternoon to interview with the hiring manager for the computer operations support team at Ames. His name was Stan Uyeda and there was not a whole lot to ask me, since I was woefully inexperienced in the computer field, but I could tell that he was desperate to fill this role. He asked me "do you have any experience with computers?" knowing full well what the answer would be. I told him no, figuring that would be the end of it, but he just sighed and said, "can you start tonight?"

It was all a blur. I was only 19 years old and never had

a real permanent job before. I figured it would be good for a while until my band got discovered and we became superstars. I would work the graveyard shift (midnight to 8:00 am), sleep during the day and rehearse with my band in the evenings before setting off for work. I could do this. How hard could it be?

You may be thinking to yourself, Computer Operator? What do you need that for? Who needs someone to operate a laptop or desktop system? Aren't they all pretty much self-operating? Of course, this was back in the days of huge mainframe computers that took up a space the size of a warehouse and had to have constant air conditioning maintained in the area or else the computers would melt, catch on fire, or who knows what else.

The IBM 360/67

My first night at the Central Computer Facility at Ames Research Center went like this: After being somewhat amazed at all of the IBM equipment in the room and taking in the oddball personalities of the crew – it was the graveyard shift, after all – I was shown what to do. This was my introduction to the IBM 360 model 67, hereafter known as the IBM 360/67. After about half an hour, all of the backlog was completed, and I remember the grave shift supervisor smiling at me and saying, "That's it. We're done for the night."

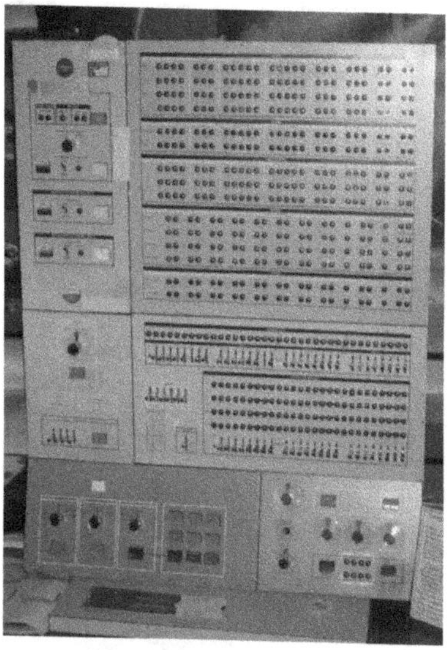

What? That was it? I was given some manuals to read for the rest of the shift, and one of the operators gave me the tour and showed me how to do the required maintenance chores, such as stock up on printer paper, clean the tape drives, and just generally get the lay of the land. Then, of course, someone was tasked with going out to bring back food for the crew. There were very few places open 24 hours, so the choices were pretty much limited to Denny's or Jack-in-the-Box. Also, of utmost importance to me, I met my future wife that night and we've been together ever since.

After that first night, the workload increased dramatically. I will attempt to describe a typical night on the graveyard shift. There was really not much thinking involved. The important thing was to be precise and accurate with each task you were performing and memorize certain steps to take in order to bring the mainframe back up once the system had crashed; and it happened quite often. These days you would expect a crashed computer to automatically reboot itself, but there was no such thing in 1972. When the computer crashed, you would not know it unless you noticed that the lights on the panel were frozen or running in a loop. Another way to

IBM punchcards

tell was to receive a phone call from a frustrated and angry engineer working in one of the wind tunnels telling us that the computer appears to be crashed because they are no longer receiving data. Thus began the operation of bringing the system back up through an intricate series of toggle switches and buttons. It was also necessary to load the operating system each and every single time from a hopefully not-too-worn punch card deck. You needed to pay attention to the console (there were no visual screens involved – just a teletype terminal that required a fan-fold box of paper to be present at all times) and respond to the prompts. Fail to do that and the system will not boot up as expected.

In the event of a hardware failure, which occurred quite often, a call would have to go out to the Customer Engineer from IBM assigned to the facility. During the day the same engineer would be on site but given that this was a 24-hour facility, there was no rest for this weary Customer Engineer. When this sort of thing happened, logs had to be filled out and phone message machines updated, and the rest of the time spent catching up on cleanup chores.

When the computer was up and running, the usual routine was to check the backlog queue for any batch jobs that were waiting to be run and submit them. There were three priorities, each costing the programmer a different charge depending on the priority submitted for the particular job. For instance, a "rush" job would cost the most, but it would ensure the batch job went to the start of the line. The other priorities were "normal" and "deferred", the latter of which were designed to run on the grave shift. What was a "batch job"? Really nothing more than a deck of punch cards, each card representing a line of code, usually COBOL or FORTRAN, fed into a card reader and written to memory in a "batch".

A typical IBM card reader.

If you are familiar with computer programming, you're probably used to writing code in a word processor sort of application; basically, any text editor, and then compiling the code into a binary executable which is then executed with a single command. Or maybe you're using a scripting language, such as Perl or Python or some other language. A typical accounting program that keeps track of payroll or other such administrative function was usually a dozen or more boxes of punch cards – each box containing, for instance, 2000 cards. Most batch jobs were somewhere around 50 to

100 cards and could be fed into the reader in a matter of minutes, provided the card reader didn't jam. In the case of a jam, the operator would try his or her best to clear the jam but failing that, put in a call to the Customer Engineer responsible for maintenance. Pity the poor CE who gets that call at 3:00 in the morning to repair a jammed card reader.

Once a batch job was created, it would go into a job queue and would be run according to how the operator set the queues up. There was some strategy in all of this where the operator was trusted to make the most logical decisions in order to get all of the backlog done before the next shift arrived. It was a sort of juggling act. That was the goal – to allow the incoming day shift, consisting entirely of government civil service workers, most always retired Navy or Army veterans trained to do the same job I was trained to do in a single night, to start off fresh, without any backlog. It was a worthy skill, but you could never use it anywhere else that I knew of, so I committed myself to the job and found that I was exceptionally good at it.

A typically large program, such as a payroll accounting job, could take up to eight hours to run. In modern terms, this would be a script or compiled machine code that would run in about thirty seconds, and if you had a syntax or some other sort of error, you would fix it immediately and run it again with success. Now picture how this was done in the good old wild west days of computers. The programmer would have a keypunch operator prepare a series of cards and rubber band them together or put them in a series of boxes if too large to hand-carry. The programmer walks into the lobby of the computer facility and submits the deck or decks of cards to an I/O (Input/Output) clerk, after first filling out a header card containing all of the required information, such as priority ("deferred" was cheapest and ideal for grave shift, since there were never any "rush" jobs left over), estimated number of seconds the job was expected to run (very useful for the operator to use some strategy as to which job queue to submit it to), and most important of all – the Job Order Table, which was the account number to charge the job to. Basically, this was similar to someone's credit card number.

Now, the programmer could either hang out and wait for

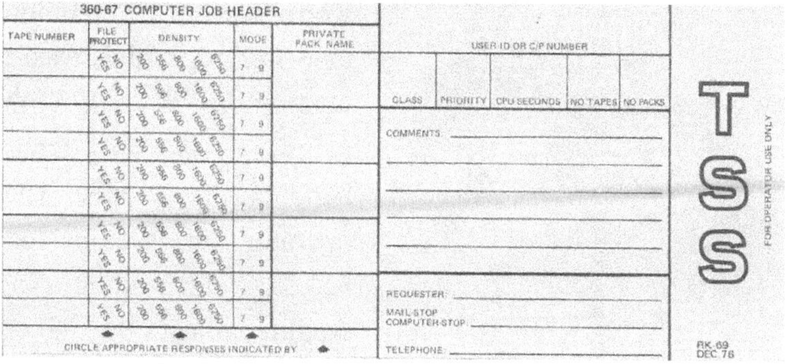

360-67 COMPUTER JOB HEADER									
TAPE NUMBER	FILE PROTECT	DENSITY	MODE	PRIVATE PACK NAME	USER ID OR C/P NUMBER				
			7 9		CLASS	PRIORITY	CPU SECONDS	NO TAPES	NO PACKS
			7 9		COMMENTS				
			7 9						
			7 9						
			7 9						
			7 9						
			7 9						
			7 9		REQUESTER				
			7 9		MAIL STOP				
					COMPUTER STOP				
CIRCLE APPROPRIATE RESPONSES INDICATED BY ◆					TELEPHONE				RK-69 DEC 76

T S S (FOR OPERATOR USE ONLY)

The job header card that was required in order to run any TSS (Time Sharing System) program on the IBM 360/67.

the output to be delivered in the form of a hardcopy (today you just stare at your screen for the results), or go out to dinner or home for the night and return later to check on the status of the job. If complete, there would be a stack, or stacks, of paper with the results of the job submitted. If you were lucky you wouldn't see a single page that said, "syntax error" and would instead see columns of figures or whatever else was expected. Today, think of a spreadsheet or PDF file that would be generated by a simple application on your desktop. As a programmer, you would repeat these steps again and again because, well because this is your job.

However, these jobs didn't always run by themselves. They were often accompanied by raw data that was necessary for the program to crunch upon. These days this data would be provided by a database or in a folder of encrypted or plain text files containing the needed data. You could keep this on a thumb drive. But back in the day, you usually provided your data on 9-track reel-to-reel tapes. These tapes were kept in a common tape library, which was a huge room in itself with racks and racks of tapes hanging side by side. The operator, or the person tasked with doing so, would collect the tapes (another item listed on the job header card that the user filled out) and gather them together on a tape cart for use during the run of the job. Here's where the operator needed to stay alert: when the console would print out a tape request, the operator had to be quick in order to make sure the job finished on time. After all, the goal was to leave no backlog for the next shift. So, after successfully mounting the tape on the device – and, like card

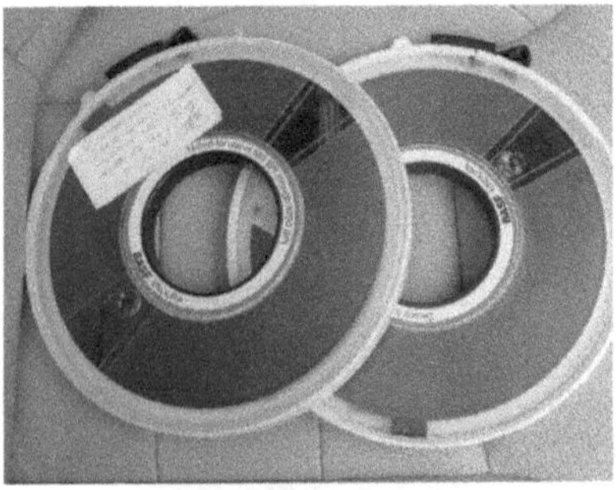

Typical 9-track reel tapes

readers and printers, there was always a possibility of something going wrong – the operator would respond to the console request with a "Y" followed by the number of the request. In the event that there was a problem mounting the tape, the job could be cancelled.

For cases where massive data was needed, disk drives were necessary. We're not talking about thumb drives or CD/DVD media. We're talking about heavy-duty canisters weighing about twenty or thirty pounds each, depending on what type of disk it was, and were usually kept in a sort of tray library. This could take up an entire room all by itself. An operator's work was often a busy one, and it could be a good workout too. It was ideally suited for young people, and indeed that's who made up the bulk of the workforce when I started out. We all could just as easily been working in the fast food industry, but instead there was this amazing job I was lucky enough to stumble upon. And I wasn't the only one. Since this work didn't require any sort of computer science degree (very few of the programmers I worked with at the time had any sort of scientific background – they were mostly in accounting or from the military), virtually any teenager looking for a job could do it, because after all; there was no one who was experienced in any of this. It was all brand new.

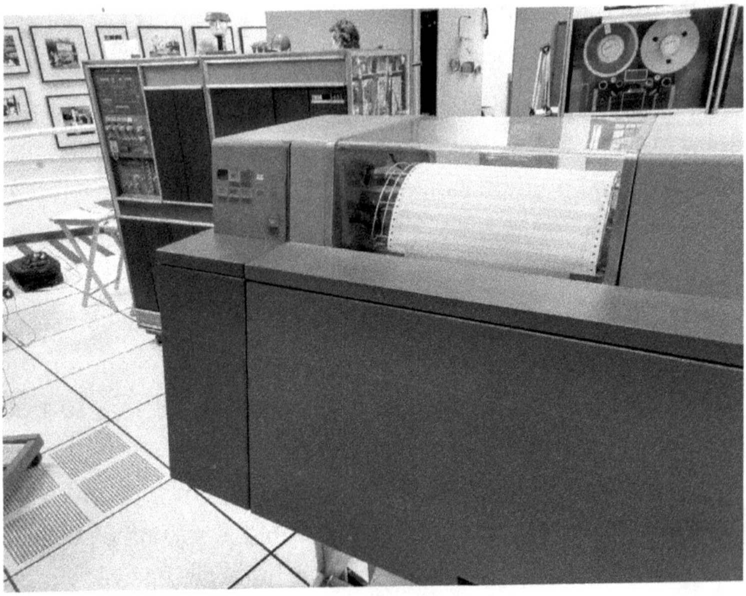

The IBM 1403 printer

Assuming the job ran successfully and required output, a print job would be submitted upon completion. We're not talking about laser or ink-jet printers (those would come later); we're talking about huge line printers using boxes of fan-fold single or multi-ply paper. Each box of paper weighed about forty pounds and one of the required operator duties was to take a trip down to the basement to load up a cart with enough paper to keep things printing throughout the shift. Loading the paper into the printer was a skill all on its own, and there was also the duty of replacing the printer ribbon when the print became faded. Unlike the simple procedure of replacing an ink cartridge in a desktop printer, this was a complicated series of steps that could easily be damaging to the printer if not done correctly. As you may imagine, being a computer operator in the beginning of the 1970s required a lot of maintenance and janitor work in addition to being able to juggle tapes and disks.

Did I mention that I worked with two IBM computers that night I started? The job actually required running two separate "twin" IBM 360/67 CPUs running two different operating systems: OS, which stood for "Operating System" and was a batch job only system, and the other was running TSS (Time Sharing System), a long forgotten real-time interactive time-sharing virtual memory operating system quite advanced for the time. But the unique thing about these two twin mainframes is that they could be combined into a single two-times-as-powerful mega system, this one running TSS, except now twice as powerful. Only the day and grave shifts could run this behemoth and it had to be reverted into two separate systems in time for the swing shift.

Did I say Behemoth? Let me give you an idea of how powerful these systems were and what the storage and memory capacity was. There were four "core boxes" in the room, each about the size of a boxcar and each containing 128 kilobytes of memory – that's right, kilobytes – adding up to a grand total of 512 kilobytes when in full duplex mode. Imagine doing anything these days with a laptop or smart phone that only holds 512 kilobytes of memory. The average file size today for just an MP3 file is around four megabytes. To get anything to work on the old IBM system required lots of swapping in and out of memory and lots of file storage on tape and disk, which had to be constantly juggled back and forth in order to retrieve the data required and store it in memory. No wonder it took so long to run a simple job that would take no more than a few seconds today.

An acoustic phone coupler used for accessing TSS.

Many programmers were able to access TSS as real-time users, in the same manner as people would use applications such as IRC (Internet Relay Chat) or Facebook. Since there was no such as thing as the Internet yet, it was possible to set up a local network – hardwired – that could be accessed through a dial-up means using what was known as an acoustic phone coupler modem, usually at a speed of no more than 300bps. Remember, all of this was cutting edge at the time. To us, it appeared that we were in the future and working with HAL9000. Today, it all seems pretty primitive, in the same way that the horse and buggy was primitive in the middle of the 20th century. All I can say is, "Get off my lawn!"

The Honeywell H200

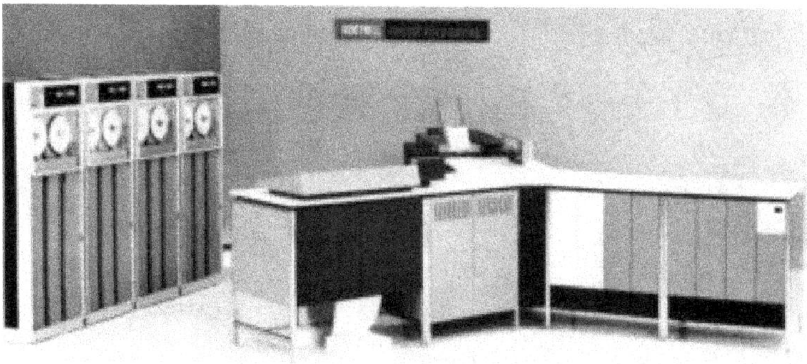

The Honeywell H200

The IBM 360 wasn't the only "big" computer at the facility. Before the 360 arrived, the wind tunnels at Ames relied on a vintage Honeywell H200. I, personally, never operated one of these, but it was just down the hall from the IBM room and I visited it quite often while I was getting acquainted with my future wife. She was the H200 operator at the time. The Honeywell H200 actually used paper tape! The wind tunnels sent their raw test data to a FlexoWriter that punched the paper tape that spilled off the machine into a roll-around cart that was taken to a winder device and wound up into tight reels, labelled and delivered to the stop box room for pickup.

I should describe how system backups were done for the IBM 360. These days, backups are usually done by simply dragging and dropping files from one device to another, say from an internal hard drive to a thumb drive or burning to a writable CD or DVD disc. Takes only a matter of minutes. Not so in the old days of mainframes. We ran a weekly job called Migration; its only function being transferring files from one media to another. Internal storage was limited and

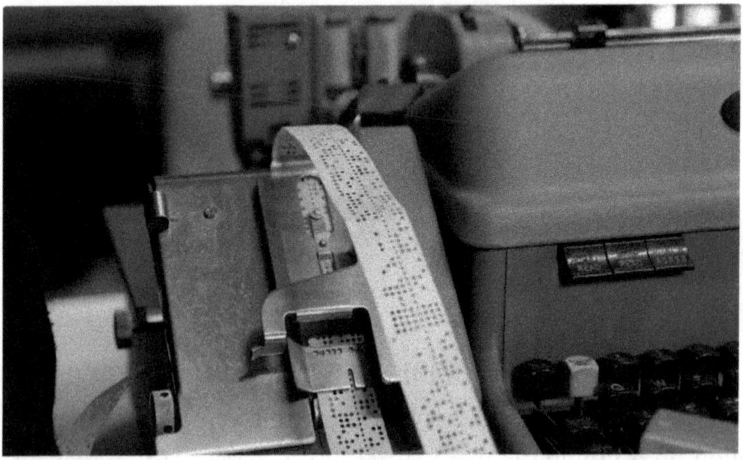

The FlexoWriter for punching paper tape used by the Honeywell H200.

temporary, and the operating system did not permanently reside in disk or memory, as it does today. You had to reload the operating system each and every time you brought it up. What was really being backed up was external user data, for instance from tape to disk and from disk to a larger storage media known as a drum. This was a time-consuming laborious procedure of saving data from tape to temporary storage in local memory and then swapping that data out to either another tape or to a "large storage" removable disc, such as an IBM 3330. This particular disk model, introduced in 1970, had a whopping 100MB of storage. The capacity of the average thumb drive these days is around 16GB. You obviously needed a lot of these disks to hold anything useful. The completed backup media was transferred offsite for safe keeping. The entire job usually lasted eight hours.

Since the Ames Central Computer Facility was primarily in support of the wind tunnels, one of which – the 80x120 tunnel, which was the largest in the world – it was of great benefit to have what were referred to as "remotes" in various buildings throughout the base so that programmers wouldn't have to travel to the main facility to submit jobs and receive output. The base didn't have networking in the sense that we know it now. There was no such thing as WiFi or any sort of broadband ethernet connections available, so all of the so-called networking was actually hardwired connections underground throughout the entire base, much the same way that electric power is provided to homes throughout your neighborhood. These remotes were equipped with some basics, such as a card reader, a printer, a teletype console, and perhaps a tape and/or disk drive. The idea was to allow the remote operator to submit and run minimal jobs that did not require lots of external data. It saved a lot of travel back and forth across the base when it may not have been necessary. True networking would come later when the DEC Vax systems were brought on board, but even then, the networking was specific to DEC systems and not

The IBM 3330 disk

as extensive as we are used to now.

The Game Changer

Shortly after I started working the grave shift at Ames, an all-hands meeting was called for all the contractors and we were given some startling news. There was a lawsuit brought by a contractor against the government alleging pay inequality between the civil service workers and contractors doing the same job. In fact, the contractors were doing much more than the civil service workers and it was decided in court that contractor pay and benefits should immediately come into line with the same pay and benefits enjoyed by the government workers. What this meant for me was that I suddenly got a huge pay raise. Instead of minimum wage, I was now getting approximately three times as much per hour as I had been getting. All of a sudden, my temporary minimum wage job turned into a real career. I put off my notion of quitting the job for a better one, because how could I possibly do better? I'm sure the same thoughts occurred to the rest of the crew, and I have no doubt that this decision greatly increased the flood of workers into the fledgling high-tech industry in the valley, even though very few of them actually had any practical experience. Again, it was all brand new.

I decided to take advantage of my proximity to computers to teach myself how to program. Starting with BASIC, I moved on to FORTRAN and studied the basic command language of the various computer systems I was fortunate to have access to, being that it was NASA and there were many local computer companies supporting the facility. Thus, the movement toward smaller and more robust digital computers, such as Digital Equipment Corporation's PDP and VAX systems, and soon to follow the Sun and Silicon Graphics (SGI) workstations, which brought visual graphics to the table. This was perfect for the aeronautics research that was taking place on the base. I was also lucky to have had first-hand experience with super computers such as the CRAY and CDC mega systems. Eventually, I left NASA to work for SGI, of which I will speak in more detail later in this book. The point is that none of what we were doing at the time required Computer Science degrees or any sort of vast knowledge of math. The only requirement was the eagerness to learn and the brains to take it all in and make sense of it.

As for Moffett Field, it was closed down as a naval air station on July 1, 1994. It was turned over to Ames Research Center and became Moffett Federal Airfield. As of this writing, Google (whose headquarters is just down the road) has a 60-year lease on 1000 acres of land on the former Naval Air Station, including the historic Hangar One, which is one of the most recognizable landmarks of Silicon Valley. At this time, it is being restored and the completion is scheduled for 2025.

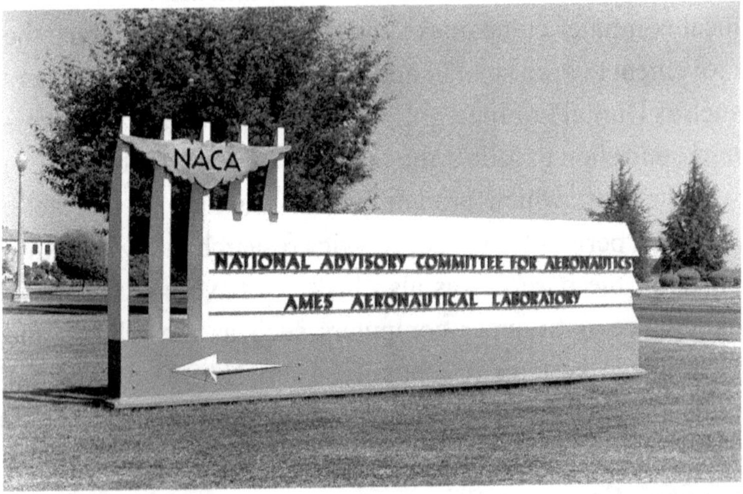

NACA at Moffett Field before it became NASA

Hangar One at Moffett Field, circa 1950s

The 80x120 wind tunnel at Ames – the largest wind tunnel in the world

The 12-foot wind tunnel at Ames, circa 1993

Top and Bottom: The author and his wife observing the reconstruction of the 12-foot tunnel.

The CDC 7600 at Ames Research Center

The CDC Cyber 205 at Ames Research Center

Seymour Cray with his Cray-1 supercomputer. Ultimately, Silicon Graphics would acquire Cray in the mid 1990s

The IBM 360 Model 67

Top and Bottom: A bit of marketing. Various models being used to sell the IBM systems to various facilities.

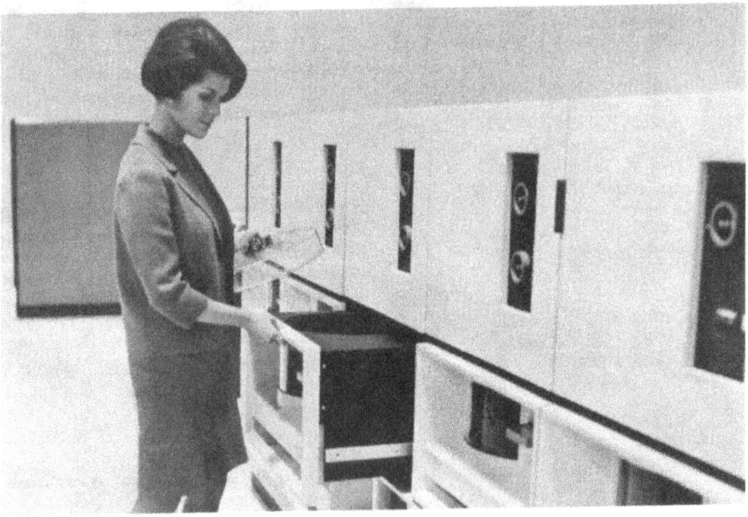

Top and Bottom: Some typical computer operations specialists using IBM equipment.

Top and Bottom: Typical IBM computer rooms of the 1970s

Air conditioning was a pretty big deal back then.

The next few pages contain pictures taken at the central computational facility at Ames Research Center in Mountain View in the mid '80s. Real shifts, real staff, real working conditions... no models were used ...

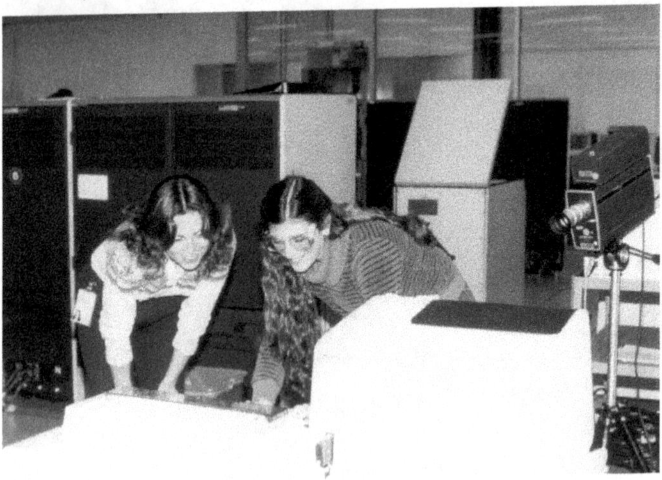

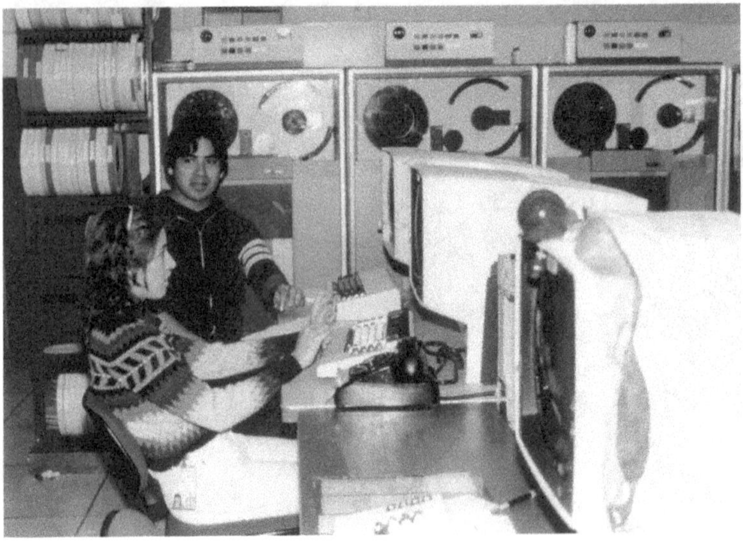

EXIT

Please
Only Destroy As Much
As You Have To

These days it's quite common to eat your lunch at your desk while working with computers, but in those days, it was considered damaging to the data. This was a poster prominently displayed in the computer room to discourage this.

Yes, smoking in the computer room was discouraged, because smoke really could cause damage to storage media, among other things. Pretty much everyone I worked with at the time smoked in the computer room, including me. Even the IBM Customer Engineers smoked in the computer room. This poster was considered to be a joke among us all.

Chapter 3: The Killer App

The Birth of the Internet

The Internet was invented, or rather developed, for one purpose only: as a means of sharing files across a great distance in a matter of minutes. That was it. No one ever dreamed of social media or streaming music or video. The developers of the Internet, i.e. the US Government, were not interested in anything other than to transfer files quickly and efficiently so that advanced research and development could commence, mainly on the space program and other scientific and military projects. E-mail was a logical next step, because the importance of quickly sharing written communication between partners was just as important as sharing files, and telephone calls were not always ideal for preserving historical information and written communication through traditional means often took too long to be efficient. Even then, in the early days of e-mail it could sometimes take nearly as long to receive an electronic message as it took to send it through regular US mail. I remember the first e-mail I sent to a friend at the University of Washington in the early '80s. It literally took two weeks for it to arrive, because the message was being sent via a now outdated method known as UUCP (Unix-to-Unix Copy Protocol). This meant that the message was delivered to a remote host running Unix and then delivered to another host and yet another until it reached its destination. I remember getting an excited phone call from my friend telling me that it arrived. We were both out of our minds with excitement due to this amazing accomplishment!

Prior to a successful network connection between various facilities, such as BBN (Bolt Beranek Newman) in Massachusetts and Stanford University in California, the method of transferring files containing data was to send them through the US or international mail on some sort of physical media, which in the 1960s and early 1970s meant punch cards or magnetic tape. That usually took days, if not weeks.

The Internet, as we know it today, is actually a collection of various different networks that were being developed in the early 1970s. There was the ARPANET (Advanced Research Projects Agency Network), MILNET (Military Network), and NSFNET (National Science Foundation Network). As a grave shift computer operator at Ames Research Center in the early 1970s, I was called upon to occasionally work with BBN in their efforts to establish a network connection between them and Ames. Many an hour I spent on the phone with a BBN engineer, operating the ARPANET TIP (Terminal Interface Processor) according to the engineer's instructions. This was the beginning of the Internet, but I sure didn't know it at the time.

In 1958 the United States Department of Defense created the Defense Advanced Research Projects Agency, or DARPA as it was originally known. The original intent of the agency was to develop new technologies for use by the military. The impetus for the creation of the agency was the space race that the US was involved in with Russia, who had just launched the satellite Sputnik. So, already the space program was behind the technologies that we now take for granted. Rather than the result of private sector innovation, as many may now mistakenly believe, it was solely a government effort to "beat the Russians" at their own game. Thus, the National Aeronautics and Space Administration, or NASA, was formed soon after and ARPA became basically an arm of NASA in their efforts to win the space race. In the late 1960s the ARPANET was created by the agency for the purpose of sharing information between various government agencies and the research institutes and universities that were assisting NASA in their efforts to put a man on the moon. It was in 1968 that BBN won the contract to develop the Internet as we know it today, although it was still in its primitive stages.

When I first became exposed to the Internet in the early 1970s, there were so few nodes connected to the network that they could all be referred to, in human terms, by a single name. For instance, the earliest hostnames I encountered were named after Star Wars or Tolkien characters, such as Vader or Frodo. Simple.

The Rise of the World Wide Web

Fast forward to the early 1990s. While I was working as a computer support engineer at NASA Ames Research Center in Moffett Field, the Internet had turned into a very useful tool for everyone involved with NASA. E-mail, file transfers, and remote connections were already common for practically everyone at the center, so it was mandated that Ames set up what was known as a Gopher server. You can look it up, but briefly it was an Internet application that was designed to share information with other nodes in a more user-friendly way. Rather than using command line notation, the user would bring up an application that featured a very crude API (Application Programming Interface) much as we are used to seeing these days, except that it was a primitive GUI (Graphical User Interface), pronounced as "gooey", that could function on a variety of devices. But the special thing that Gopher did was to present a store of information (files) that could be accessed or downloaded to the user's local host machine. It was an information sharing utility that was much more advanced than most file sharing systems at the time, such as FTP (File Transfer Protocol) servers that required the user to be much more technically savvy than the average user. The advantage of Gopher was that the user could search a file hierarchy in a much simpler way. Gopher was, in a way, the direct antecedent to the World Wide Web. There were other similar services, such as WAIS (Wide Area Information Server), but Gopher was the one that Ames was most interested in.

So, I was assigned to a team that was tasked with setting up the first Gopher server at Ames. The software for setting up and maintaining Gopher was free from NCSA (National Center for Supercomputing Applications). Everything was going smoothly. We had the server up and running, with documents for sharing provided by the researchers and scientists, and tests were going well. We were ready to unveil it to management when we were suddenly taken in a new direction. By the time we had completed our setup, the World Wide

Web[4] was already beginning to be established, and it was clearly a superior solution for anyone with access to a graphic terminal capable of running NCSA Mosaic. This was the very first truly functional WWW browser, and it was stunning to see a graphical representation of the data one would be interested in downloading. Anyone who has used any of the modern-day commercial browsers, such as Chrome or Safari, knows how essential it all is. Thus, WWW became the first Internet Killer App. This was the application that was going to draw the ordinary consumer to the net, much in the same way that VisiCalc was the Killer App that convinced the consumer to purchase a PC. Up until the point where the World Wide Web became a reality, there was no real compelling reason for anyone outside of the scientific community to go to the trouble of buying and using a home computer. The idea was absurd. "What do I need that for?"; "Where would I put it? Aren't computers huge?" These would be typical questions asked by anyone outside of the technical world.

And so, our task was modified to concentrate on the WWW server instead of Gopher. This was all new territory to us. None of us knew how to set up a truly great web server, but we were sure eager to try. The results, as you might

---

[4] English scientist Tim Berners-Lee invented the World Wide Web in 1989. He wrote the first web browser in 1990 while employed at CERN near Geneva, Switzerland. CERN is a French acronym for European Organization for Nuclear Research.

imagine, were primitive. It was as simple as "here's a link to click on" with maybe a picture or two to make it all look cool. Thus, I became a webmaster in a brand-new world. Soon, services such as Netcom, CompuServe, and America Online (AOL) brought regular people to the table and gave birth to what we now know as "social media." One of the things that made these early services so compelling was Usenet, which still exists today. It was a sort of precursor to Facebook and Twitter. There were also early precursors of instant messaging apps that foresaw what we now know of as texting. Applications such as IRC and AOL's Instant Messenger were very popular at the time. E-mail, of course, was also a big game changer and continues to be relied upon very heavily.

One thing the Internet revolution brought to the computer world was the problem of security. For the first time, government and university computers had to deal with the possibility of people hacking into their systems and potentially causing damage and stealing data. This was not something NASA had been concerned with before, so an effort was made to train computer support personnel to spot break-ins and fight against hackers using their own techniques. I, myself, was sent to a training seminar on how to spot and deal with hackers by receiving tips and training from real-life hackers who were tasked with teaching techniques for gaining unauthorized access to computers using commonly overlooked aspects of system setup. All it took was for one inattentive system administrator to ignore the common pitfalls of system security and all hell could break loose. These were government computers, after all. No telling what sort of damage could be done.

Of special interest is Dan Farmer, the author of COPS, which stands for Computer Oracle and Password System. Farmer developed this suite of security vulnerability scanners in 1989 and System Administrators found it very useful when computers became accessible to the entire world and not just in a local environment, which was what COPS was designed for. Dan Farmer became something of a celebrity in the cyber world and was eventually hired by SGI to be their security expert. When I left NASA-Ames to work for SGI in 1994, they prided themselves on their record of never having a break-in due to their tight security. In fact, the security was so tight that SGI made a policy of allowing free root access[5] to every user on the SGI campus. When I mentioned this to some of my old Ames colleagues, the reaction was always "So that's why they ship their workstations without any security. It's not a problem for them!"

While working for SGI, Farmer wrote his much more advanced security penetration suite called SATAN, which stands for Security Administrator Tool for Analyzing Networks. This was quite a controversial acronym that got him into trouble and ultimately got him fired. It seems that the software suite was misunderstood by law enforcement officials as a deliberate tool for hackers to identify vulnerable computers to hack into. It was nothing of the kind and it was

[5] The user with all privileges and complete access to the system was called "root", also known as the "superuser".

never intended to be the purpose, but nevertheless SGI freaked out and let him go. He was ahead of his time, though, because shortly after his firing the tools he developed became widely used to help prevent security break-ins.

The revolution that began in 1994 continues to this day. For better or for worse.

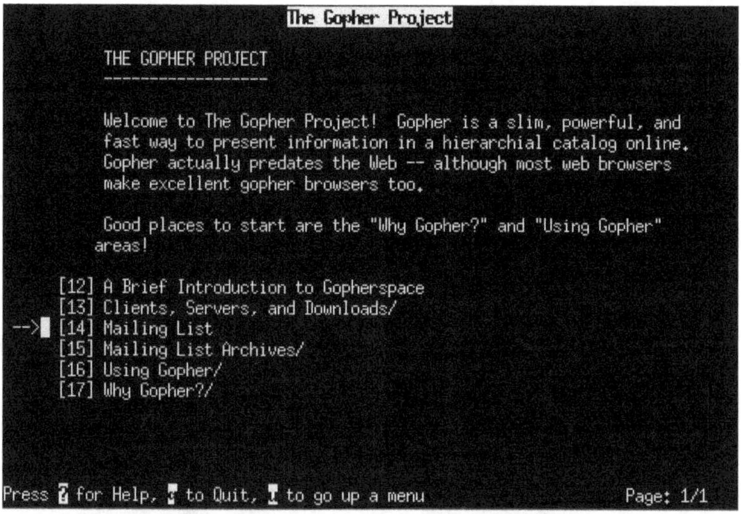

The original text-only version of Gopher

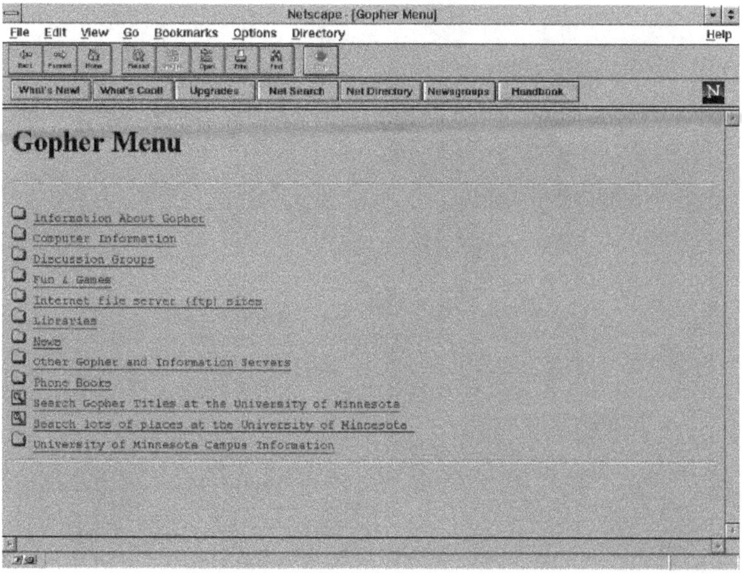

A Gopher site accessed with the then new World Wide Web

NCSA Mosaic – the first web browser

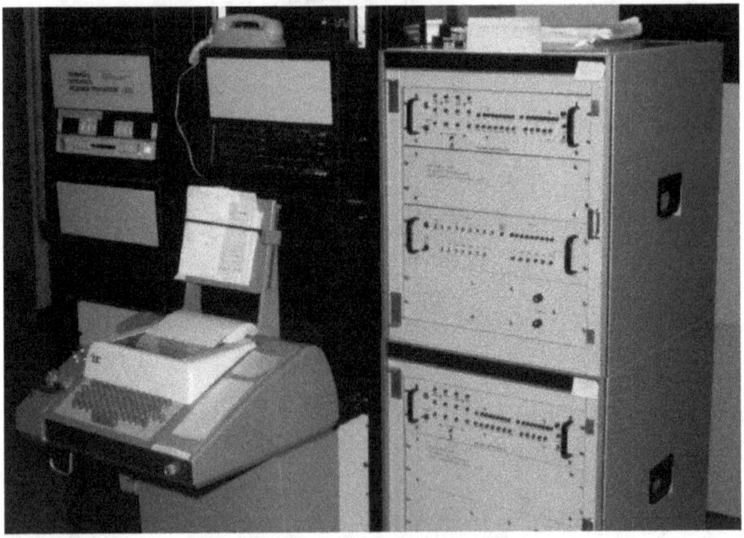

The ARPANET TIP (Terminal Interface Processor)

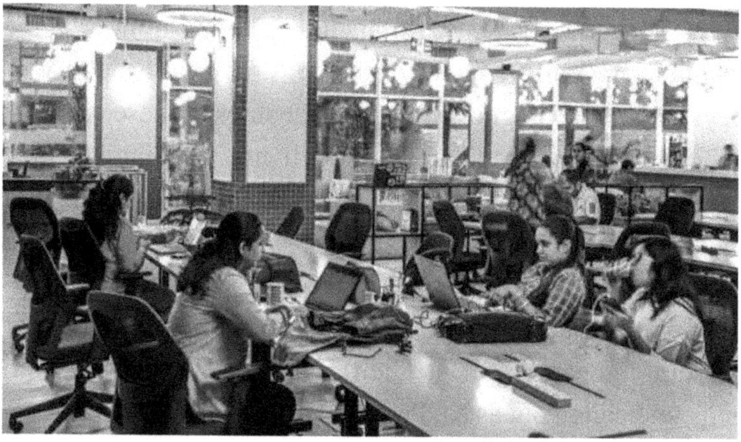

Chapter 4: Startup Fever

With the Internet in full swing after the advent of the World Wide Web, the public at large began purchasing home computers and using ISPs (Internet Service Providers) such as America Online and CompuServe, as well as using work computers now connected to the net. This presented a great opportunity for private companies to start up their own net-related businesses. Naturally, profit was the motive, now that science and research was no longer the dominant reason for using a computer. It was now for entertainment and purchasing goods, as well as keeping in touch with friends and family through e-mail and personal websites, thanks to hosting providers such as GeoCities.

Starting in 1995 and continuing up until 2000, the Dot-

Com boom began. This led to a large number of startup companies eager to make use of this new exciting frontier in the Santa Clara Valley, soon to be better known as Silicon Valley. You may recognize some of the names of these startups: Google, Yahoo, Amazon (although not a Silicon Valley startup). Others you may not have heard about, although at the time they gained great publicity and public recognition: Pets.com, Webvan, Lycos. There was even a startup company called Startups, whose main purpose was to help other startup companies get on their feet. Some were just plain silly and called out as so. Pets.com was one that seemed particularly ridiculous at the time, and so it failed. However, some of these startups were just ahead of their time. Probably every pet owner knows about the current Chewy.com, which serves the same purpose as Pets.com did, so why did it fail? Why did so many of the startups fail? One reason could just be over-saturation of the market. The public was just not ready, technologically, for the onslaught of startups, but workers in the Silicon Valley certainly were. There were suddenly a tremendous number of jobs available, and many people travelled from other states to strike gold in the Dot-Com gold rush of the late '90s. The over-saturation of the market led ultimately to the Dot-Bomb of 2000, where many of these newly relocated workers lost their jobs in a flurry of layoffs. I was one of them.

What came out of the Dot-Bomb was essentially a weeding out of some of the weaker startups and the biggest players rose to the surface. Google and Yahoo, for instance, wound up dominating the search engine market, and even Yahoo got into trouble once Google became the brand name that defines the service it provides. When was the last time someone said, "let me Yahoo that for you"? Who remembers Lycos, Magellan, Ask Jeeves, InfoSeek and numerous other search engines that were all competing with each other? They were all essentially the same, but the market didn't really need all those search engines. But for a while, all of these startups served as a training ground for new hires who essentially were brand new to all of this new technology. It was a buyer's market. The new companies needed workers and were willing to hire anyone who had the curiosity to learn, along with everybody else, how to innovate in what was essentially a brand-new world of modern technology. This, again, is where I come in.

The Dot-Com Gold Rush

The story I am about to tell was typical of what was happening during the great Dot-Com boom. By 1995, the valley was used to established and growing companies such as Sun Microsystems, Silicon Graphics, Adobe, Apple, Fairchild and Lockheed leading the way and providing employment to many up and coming computer professionals, such as myself. But with the growth of the Internet and the home computer market in bloom, people working at these established companies realized that they could start their own small companies and expand on the great technologies that were all brand new and innovative. With the help of venture capital, numerous startups were established, many of which are still with us today and many more that have vanished without a trace. The lure of these startups was, in no small part, due to stock options that were potentially very lucrative. Talk about a windfall. Stock option grants were a great way to lure new talent to a startup, and the risk was small for the worker. More often than not, the company offering the stock options failed to be successful and the options became worthless. But at least it was no cost to the worker. The most common reaction was to shrug and move on to the next startup. Many joked about the worthless stock option certificates being used as wallpaper. But when a startup had a successful public offering, such as with Google or Yahoo, the result could have been tremendous. I knew quite a few people who used their new-found wealth to purchase expensive properties, travel the world, or just simply enjoy an early retirement.

The new startups were similar to the gold mining prospectors of the previous century. Gold was to be found in the new Internet, and established companies were in need of other companies to provide services. In a similar way that gold rush towns sprang up to support the miners with food and supplies, the need was established for what became known as B-to-B companies. Business-to-Business, not something directly consumer related.

This was another "can you start tonight" moment. In my second year working for SGI in Mountain View, California, I was contacted by some ex-SGI people about possibly joining their new startup venture called CyberSource. Actually, I had checked them out earlier and passed. At that time, they were headquartered (if you can call it that) in Menlo Park near Palo Alto, a new hotbed for technology startups. The entire facility consisted of a single room with makeshift desks all crowded into each other. It didn't look too inviting, especially after having the luxury of working for an established tech company with a huge budget and Hollywood rock stars visiting every now and then. Plus, the job was doing what I had already been doing (system administration), and I figured if I was going to do the same work, I might as well keep doing it at SGI. This time was different, however. They wanted a software developer for their core group of engineers. I only dabbled in programming, and fairly rudimentary at that. In other words, I had no real experience for the job at hand, but that didn't stop them from making me an offer.

Prior to working for SGI, I was a computer support specialist at NASA Ames Research Center and had been given plenty of opportunity to learn new technologies and to be able to deal with a number of different clients with different needs. My lack of experience in all of these new technologies was not an issue. Very few people had any sort of practical experience with all the new things happening, so I just happened to be there, that's all.

At that time, the notion of purchasing products over the Internet was new, and it appeared to me that it was the wave of the future. Amazon was just a small but growing company at the time, but they definitely showed the way and I wanted to be a part of it. CyberSource was basically a credit card processing service whose primary usefulness was the ability to do instant fraud checking using artificial intelligence algorithms to determine how likely it was that the person using the credit card was really the person who owned the card. Using a set of variables, such as frequency of card usage (many rapid attempts in a very short period of time would be suspect), time of day (how likely was it that someone would be buying something online at 2:00AM in the morning in Germany), and of course the usual expiration dates and such. This was in the days before security codes on the back of the card, so there were a lot of ways that bandits could fool the system. CyberSource did a pretty good job and pretty soon added Amazon to its roster of clients. One major client I recall working with was Playboy. We all got freebies because of that. Don't get too excited, the freebies consisted of nothing more than a couple of CD-ROMs, one being an archive of Playboy interviews and the other being a sort of electronic Playmate calendar. Okay, maybe they gave us all (including the women) a copy of the latest issue.

From there, the company just got bigger and bigger, and pretty soon we were in a huge complex in Mountain View, just down the street from SGI. In fact, the building we were in was formerly owned by SGI. I was among the first twenty or so employees, but by this time the company had increased a hundred-fold at least.

What did I know about e-commerce (which wasn't even

a term yet)? Nothing. I remember interviewing for the job with the CEO of the young company (something that would likely never happen today) and being asked what I thought about the business model of CyberSource. My answer was absolutely honest, and no doubt helped me land the job. I said, "I believe that buying things over the Internet is here to stay." Just that clumsy. The CEO smiled and nodded. Other than the founders of the company, no one really knew much about e-commerce. We were all learning it as we went along!

So, I learned on the job. I had already fooled around with Perl, a then-popular scripting language that was considered ideal for dealing with the Web, and it was in that direction that I found myself headed. Later, we would switch to Java, and we all got free classes in order to learn something new. It was fun and it was nice to be able to see instant results of your coding. The other nice thing about being in this startup was the camaraderie. We were all young and learning new technologies that were fun and exciting. And no one questioned whether or not we were up to the task at hand. The other exciting element was the stock option grants that were very generous and forthcoming. We all looked forward to the day that we would do our IPO (Initial Public Offering) and all become rich beyond our wildest dreams.

Happily, for me, CyberSource did a successful IPO and we were rewarded for our hard work and determination. Eventually, CyberSource was acquired by Visa, which drove the stock price even higher. It was the only startup I was involved in that was actually successful. Subsequent to my tenure at CyberSource, I joined other startups, but they were derailed by the great Dot-Bomb of 2000. Everyone jumped on the Dot-Com bandwagon, with a bunch of oddball startups that were sometimes ahead of their time (Pets.com anyone?). Some companies grew too large too fast. CyberSource was one of them. I experienced my very first layoff in 2000, but that didn't stop me from moving on to yet another job that I was barely qualified for. That was another one of those "can you start tonight" moments, because the job I interviewed for, at XO Communications (a new merger of Concentric Networks and NextLink) required a PHP[6] programmer, and I had never even heard of this fairly new language. In fact, it was so new that there wasn't even a book that I could find to teach me how to code in that language. Knowing full well that I had never programmed in PHP, I was hired anyway because they were willing to take a chance and my track record was pretty good by that time. I seriously doubt anything like that could happen today. I ended up staying with XO for ten years and it was the best job I ever had. These days, PHP is the primary scripting language for use with the World Wide Web. I continued to program primarily in PHP until I retired from the business.

After the Crash

The startup boom was finished by 2001. George W.

---

[6] PHP is an acronym that doesn't really stand for anything, although it is used to stand for Personal Home Page.

Bush had just been elected President in a very contentious election[7] and the economy proceeded to crash. President Clinton had left office with not only a balanced budget, but with a healthy surplus. Bush destroyed all of that, and Silicon Valley reacted to that in a very negative way. We were suddenly back to the era of huge deficits. As previously mentioned, the company I was working with at the time proceeded to lay off about 20% of its employees, of which I was one. Many other companies followed suit, and many more just completely disappeared.

But the technology continued and slowly began to grow again. By this time, more and more companies were becoming pickier about who they hired. They also discovered the benefits of outsourcing and offshoring. Contractors became more common, and many of those contractors were either on a temporary basis with V1 visas or working from outside of the US. Using contractors instead of regular fulltime employees was a cost-saving measure, because contractors did not get benefits or any of the perks normally associated with high-tech companies. Good for the company but bad for the workers. Instead of feeling like you have a stake in something, contractors had no real reason to deliver quality or be innovative. More attention was now being paid to academic credentials because, frankly, the people now running things

---

[7] Bush lost the popular vote but barely won the battleground state of Florida, which pretty much decided the election once the Supreme Court stepped in and stopped the recount which would likely have gone to opponent Al Gore.

didn't know talent from one person to another. They only knew what they could see on a résumé. Candidate A had a master's degree in computer science whereas candidate B didn't have a degree, but that candidate did have twenty years of practical experience in the industry. Who are you going to go with? More often than not, the candidate chosen was the one with the credentials. They must be smart, right?

Fortunately, there were still growing and established companies that knew the value of homegrown talent, and so I was still able to work in some pretty interesting jobs and continue to increase my knowledge of technology. Unfortunately, however, much of the technology used by these companies was stale and lacking in innovation or imagination. We began to see a consolidation of technologies blended down into one giant company hogging the space once occupied by a number of different companies working the same issues. For example, the search engine space was originally designed to make better use of the fledgling World Wide Web so that users, most often computer professionals, could easily find the information they were looking for and see it presented in a friendly and useful manner. In this space we had Yahoo, Lycos, Magellan, Infoseek, Ask Jeeves, Altavista, and numerous others. Then along comes Google. They were just another search engine, but they managed to do it a little better and provided extra services beyond just surfing the Web. But Yahoo was doing the same and provided a popular e-mail service for novices who had no idea how to use e-mail, which was also something Google excelled at. Ultimately, Google prevailed, and the rest just vanished, except for Yahoo which continues to struggle to this day in the shadow of Google.

Amazon is another example of consolidation. The battle for online sales – in the case of Amazon it was books and CDs – was ultimately won by Amazon. Why? Better marketing and name recognition. Also, they bought up smaller competing companies, thus eliminating their competition. I remember being a loyal customer of CDNow, which was where I bought all of my CDs online, but when Amazon acquired them, I had little choice but to switch to Amazon.

These are just two examples. And with the consolidation and elimination of serious competition came the thought that innovation was no longer necessary. Neither was quality control. When you're the big boy on the block, who's going to tell you what you can and can't do? It's all about monetizing everything through advertising these days. This was *not* what the founders of Silicon Valley had in mind.

Another thing that ruined the Internet, in my opinion, was the rise of plug-ins and frameworks that just about anyone could use, but still the thought was that only accredited computer science geniuses would understand these rather unimaginative building blocks more often than not replete with bugs that no one had any interest in fixing or improving. Added to that, the commercial aspects of the Internet made it desirable for web designers to put as many obtrusive advertising widgets on a page so that it ultimately became useless and unusable. Again, not something envisioned by the founding fathers of Silicon Valley.

More often than not, these days, we see "upgrades" and "improvements" to applications that no one asked for or needed. The changes are made just to keep up the appearance that programmers are busy at work. Back in the old days, changes to application design were only done out of necessity, and if something was already working well, no need to change things. Again, I say "get off my lawn!"

The most popular aspect of the Internet, as of this writing anyway, has to be social media. In my opinion, Steve Jobs didn't do us any favors by creating and marketing the iPhone. It wasn't the first smart phone, but it was the Killer App that kickstarted the whole social media phenomenon.

The Rise of Social Media

As previously mentioned, in the early days of the Internet, there was a pioneering social media application called Usenet. This was a text-only application used by computer professionals to share information and hold discussions in "newsgroups", which is similar to today's groups on Facebook. A typical newsgroup might be interested in the topic of cooking or a favorite musician or musical group. Like the World Wide Web of today, the groups were divided into hierarchies with the main group being something like "talk", "news", "rec", "sci", etc. At first, there was really only one main group: "net", so that you would have a group like net.music – a very vague and overly generic place where people could discuss music. Naturally, a group like net.music would become confusing and chaotic when you have users who wanted to discuss classical music and others who wanted to discuss the Beatles. Not only that, but the designation of "net" meant very little in the way of distinguishing the type of discussion group you wanted to create, and it was very easy to create a group (I did it myself for Bob Dylan when I drove the creation of a group devoted to him. It still exists today). Someone, somewhere, decided that if you were going to create a new group, it should fall into the appropriate category. Therefore, discussions of a recreational nature, as opposed to scientific or government or location related topics, would fall under the "rec" main group. Thus, musically related discussion groups such as rec.music.beatles or rec.music.dylan (a group I helped create) existed and were very popular for discussing those artists. Scientific groups such as sci.agriculture or sci.anthropology existed for the purpose of discussing those particular scientific fields.

But the limitations of such a technology were obvious. You had no way to link articles together in a visual way, and there was no way to display anything visual. It was all text oriented. There was also the big problem of a lack of transparency. One could be completely anonymous when using Usenet, and this didn't always make for polite conversation and oftentimes led to hostility known as "flame wars". Many people joined Usenet with the sole intention of stirring up trouble and took great delight in causing friction in the various groups. These people were called "trolls", and it is a term which is still commonly used to this day[8]. During the 2016 election, Russian hackers interfered with the election by way of what was commonly referred to as "troll farms". It was through Usenet that this concept first appeared. Ultimately, many users, including myself, left Usenet because of this and sought greener pastures. Those greener pastures included the more visual and robust mediums of MySpace and Facebook, which overtook MySpace to become the de facto social media app that most everyone has been drawn to. Facebook started life as Facemash when Mark Zuckerberg and fellow students at Harvard wanted a web application designed to rate women based on their looks. Eventually, this silly app became something much larger when Zuckerberg established his operation in the heart of Silicon Valley, Menlo Park, where the corporate headquarters still resides today.

But the importance of Usenet and subsequent real-time chat apps such as IRC to the software developers of Silicon Valley cannot be understated. These primitive methods of connecting together the various groups of individuals that would drive the technology that we are now familiar with went a long way toward providing a sense of community that is now largely missing from the industry. It is doubtful whether or not Facebook, and similar platforms such as Twitter and Instagram, would have gained the sort of traction

---

[8] Contrary to what many may think, the term has nothing to do with the mythical creature hiding under a bridge ready to grab unsuspecting victims, but rather a reference to the fishing practice of trolling, whereby a fisherman throws a line in the water and moves along in a boat hoping to catch whatever happens to take the bait.

they would have now if it were not for Usenet and IRC. Of course, the real impetus for the success of social media has to go to Steve Jobs at Apple who drove the popularity of what we now refer to as the smart phone. Time will tell if this technology will be seen as a curse or a blessing to humanity.

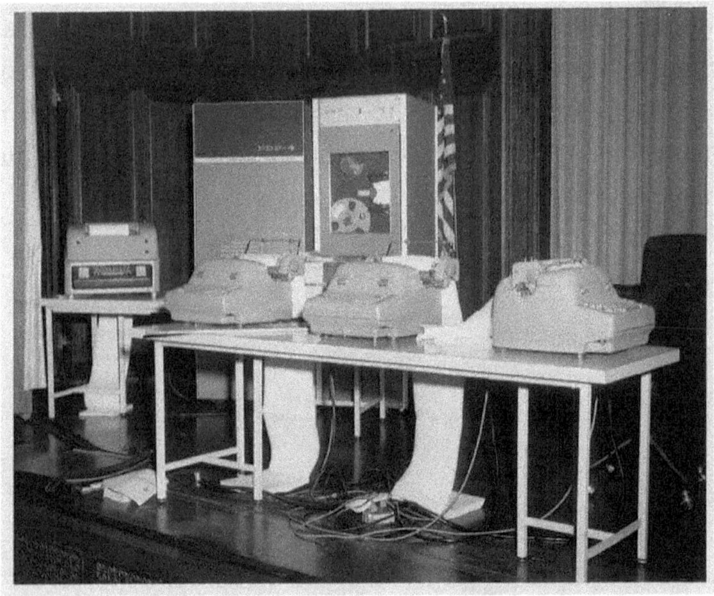

Chapter 5: Five Forgotten Giants of Silicon Valley

For every Facebook and Google there are a hundred failed startups that no one remembers. But there's a small number of forgotten companies that were big. HUGE. They were giants in the Valley, and everyone who was anyone in the computer field in the Bay Area knew of or worked with these companies. Chances are, anyone under 40 years old will have no idea who these companies are and why they were at one time exceedingly important.

Digital Equipment Corporation

This may seem like cheating because Digital Equipment Corporation, hereafter referred to as DEC, was not located in the Silicon Valley. It was based in Maynard, Massachusetts, but its impact was felt very strongly in Silicon Valley and California in general, especially at NASA installations and universities. It was at one time considered to be the #2 computer company after IBM. As an example of how important DEC was to the Valley, there was a western headquarters located in the city of Santa Clara, wherein a number of classes were available to computer specialists working in the area, of which I was one. Their customer base was worldwide, but in the Bay Area they were absolutely essential. Every year the DEC Users' Society, or DECUS, put on symposiums in various locations. DEC employees would attend and lead panels and give presentations of importance to programmers and managers utilizing DEC computers in their jobs. These conferences mostly acted as a perk to computer professionals, because they were often held in cities like Las Vegas or San Diego, where there was access to vacation funtime activities. I went to a few myself, and they were indeed fun. You got to meet a lot of interesting people and shared a lot of knowledge and tricks of the trade.

In the 1980s, DEC created and marketed the mini-computer. This was a new development which tended to make super mainframes, such as those produced by IBM, somewhat archaic. The minicomputers were versatile and perhaps a little more affordable than the super computers most facilities were then using. DEC's PDP (Programmed Data Processor) series, of which the PDP-1 was the first (in 1959), were extremely important in the world of computers.

The even more successful PDP-5 followed, eventually leading to the PDP-11 on which computer scientists at the University at Berkeley developed their own version of Unix[9], an operating system that dominates today (MacOS is Unix based) and eventually crushed DEC's own proprietary OS.

When I first started working at Ames on the graveyard shift, PDPs were in use, although not by me. I didn't really see my first DEC system until I started working with the VAX (Virtual Address eXtension), which was a more advanced and more sophisticated minicomputer that was ideal for replacing the central IBM system that research engineers were working with at the time. It was also ideal for networking and timesharing. The VMS (Virtual Memory System) operating system was very advanced for its time and was quite popular with programmers and System Managers (now

---

[9] The development of Unix began in 1969 at Bell Labs by Ken Thompson, Dennis Ritchie and others.

called System Administrators). It certainly rivalled, if not surpassed, IBM's timesharing TSS operating system. One of the attractions of the VMS operating system was the ability to interact with other users through real-time messaging and e-mail. It also featured a nice network system called DECnet that connected various VAX systems throughout the country, although in a much more limited manner than the Internet itself. It also featured its own version of a network file system whereby multiple VAX systems could be clustered together in order to form a robust local area network.

The main console interface to the computer was a hardcopy Teletype-like terminal, but operators and programmers more often used remote CRT terminals developed by DEC. The VT100 was a more advanced version of the VT52, which was in use by the PDP systems. The VT100 had more features and was pretty good at displaying data in a crudely graphical screen.

Using the VT100, an operator could enter commands using DCL (Digital Command Language), which was almost a conversational way to interact with the system to get information or tell it what to do. But the real strength in DCL was its use as a programming language to allow the user to run scripts, sometimes very lengthy and complicated scripts utilizing standard IF-THEN-ELSE and similar programming constructs. It was my first real exposure to system programming, and it came in handy when I decided to switch careers and go into programming instead of continuing with computer support (I could see where that path was heading, and it didn't look very promising). In the 1980s it was a very popular language indeed. Today, very few people have heard of it, no doubt.

In a way, DEC's popularity gave rise to their downfall. The proprietary VMS operating system was overwhelmed by the freely available Unix operating system – developed on DEC's PDP-11 mini-computers! They actually provided the platform which eventually spelled their doom. As previously mentioned, the Unix-based operating system is in wide use today, especially by Apple and Oracle, among many others. To try to compete with this, DEC developed their own version of the Unix operating system called Ultrix, which ran on their own platform. They also attempted to stem their decline by developing new systems, such as the VAX 9000 and the DEC Alpha, a RISC (Reduced Instruction Set Computer) architecture that was designed to compete in the burgeoning server market, but it was too little too late.

The DEC Alpha server

After floundering for a while, DEC was purchased in 1998 by Compaq, a company known mainly for their PC workstations. Eventually, Compaq merged with Hewlett-Packard in 2002.

Believe it or not, there are still many computer installations continuing to use the VAX/VMS systems that were acquired way back when it was the big boy on the block. These are mostly Government installations slow to modernize. A number of computer support companies exist purely to support the still-running DEC systems. I was surprised to find one of them in the small town in Oregon where I currently live, far outside of Silicon Valley.

Digital founder Ken Olsen

PDP-11

DEC Users' Society, or DECUS, as it was known. This organization would put on a yearly symposium for DEC enthusiasts.

Top and Bottom: The two flagship VAXes – the VAX 11/780 and the VAX 11/750

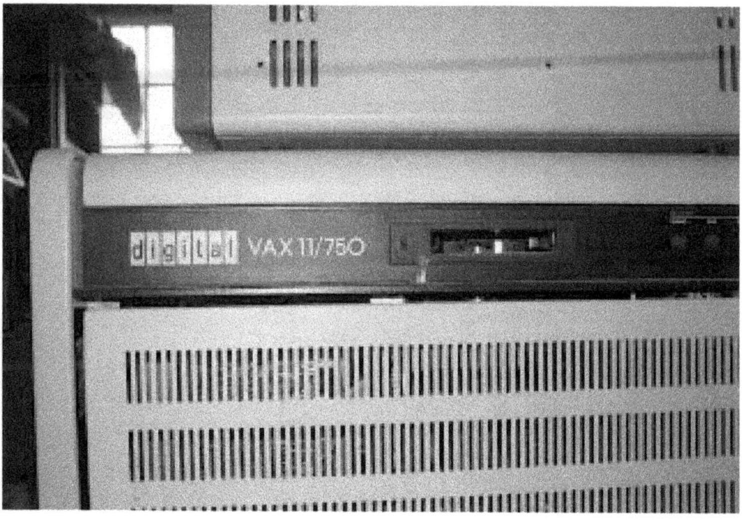

Typical VT100 from the 1980s

The VAX 11-780-5

The PDP-1, first released in 1959

The PDP-1 development team

Silicon Graphics

Silicon Graphics Incorporated (herein after referred to as SGI) was founded in Mountain View, California, in 1981 by James H. Clark after leaving his position as a professor of electrical engineering at Stanford University (there's that Stanford connection again), along with some graduates at Stanford and others in the valley. What was significant about SGI was the emergence of 3D graphics workstations, which was uniquely suited to Space Science research going on at various NASA installations, such as NASA-Ames Research Center just down the road at Moffett Field in Mountain View. Ames Research Center was one of the biggest customers for the new SGI, and it was at Ames that I saw my first SGI workstation. I couldn't believe what I was seeing. I didn't realize at the time how lucky I was to be able to work with a number of SGI systems in a computer support capacity. At the time, I was still focused on VAX/VMS, having become a System Manager for a bunch of VAX systems being used by the Army in their helicopter division. The SGI systems were being groomed as a replacement for the VAX systems, along with some other workstation options such as Sun Microsystems and Apollo workstations.

I remember being immediately impressed by some of the software available on the first SGI system I ever encountered: the IRIS 1400, first released in 1984. Of special interest was the flight simulator and some of the graphic creation utilities such as Adobe's Photoshop and Illustrator, which came standard on the platform, written in SGI's proprietary Unix system called IRIX. It was also the first time I encountered the game DOOM. Many an off-hour was spent among engineers playing this game. It was just one of many.

The SGI IRIS workstation.

The Indigo

In 1987, SGI was the first to use the RISC (Reduced Instruction-Set Chip) architecture from MIPS (which actually stands for Millions of Instructions Per Second), which SGI would eventually acquire. But it was the Indigo that really put SGI on the map. It was more along the lines of a personal computer with massive 3D graphic capabilities. It was truly state-of-the-art. By the time I started working for SGI, the standard workstation used by most people was the Indy. It was more affordable and very user-friendly. It was around this time that Hollywood came to call.

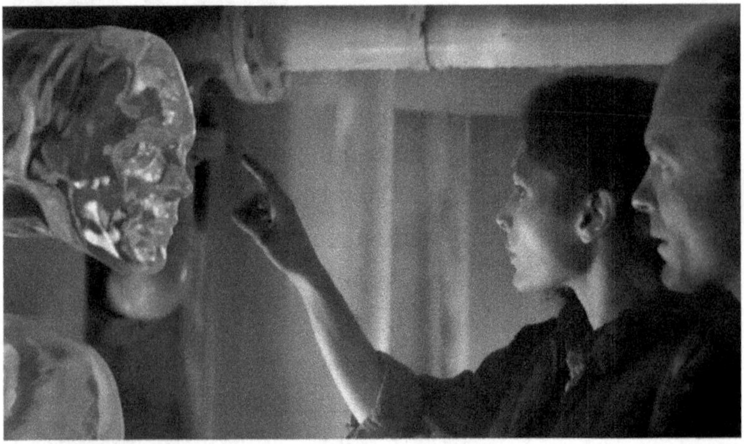

Scene from James Cameron's 1989 film The Abyss. The first film to present SGI's morphing technology.

In 1993 Silicon Graphics teamed up with Industrial Light and Magic to revolutionize the special effects seen in movies. Prior to this, most special effects that you would see in the movies would likely be stop-motion animation, such as we were familiar with from films such as *King Kong* and *The 7th Voyage of Sinbad*, most famously created by Ray Harryhausen. Industrial Light and Magic had been using SGI technology since 1987, but it wasn't really until 1989, when James Cameron released *The Abyss*, that the public came to see the future of special effects in film. It was the first time the public had seen what was initially described as "morphing" in the movies. No amount of stop-motion animation could create the effects that were witnessed by filmgoers when that film was released.

The film was something of a disappointment at the box office, however, and received mixed reviews, although it did win an Academy Award for best special effects. Cameron followed it up with a much more extensive use of SGI's technology with *Terminator 2* in 1991, which was a tremendous box office success and, up to that time, the greatest special effects film anyone had ever seen. But it was Steven Spielberg's *Jurassic Park* in 1993 that put the final nail in the coffin of traditional stop-motion animation. Anyone who saw the movie when it was first released was no doubt astounded by what they were witnessing on the screen. These days it's a pretty much ho-hum affair to see such visuals, but in the early 1990s it was something to behold. And it was all due to Silicon Graphics.

Again, this is where I come in.

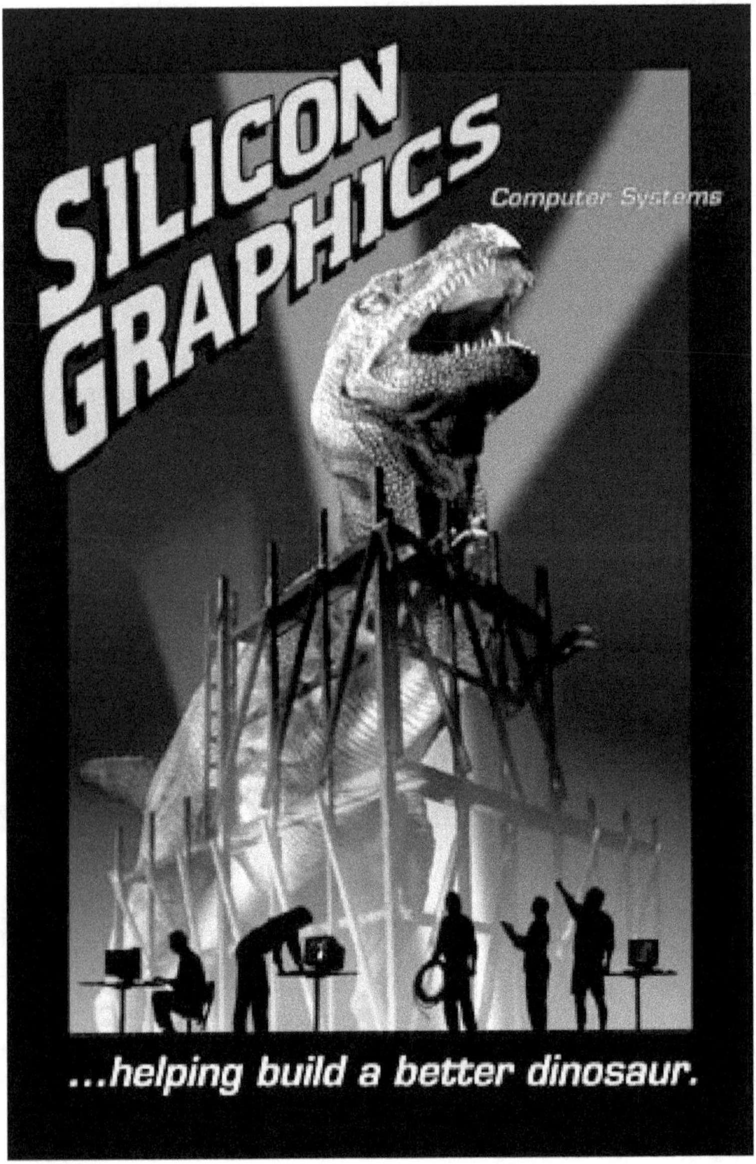
SILICON GRAPHICS
Computer Systems
...helping build a better dinosaur.

Jurassic Park was such a huge success, that SGI found itself in the enviable position of being able to expand exponentially on the world stage. Suddenly, they needed to hire thousands of new workers to handle the demand that Hollywood was placing on the now incredibly successful Silicon Valley startup. In 1995, in another one of those "can you start tonight" moments for me, some ex-Ames employees, now working for SGI, were in desperate need of a system administrator for one of their departments, the Software Licensing and Software Distribution arm of the company. They were located off-campus at the time, but ultimately moved to the main campus. I was, of course, intrigued at the offer, but thought they might want to interview me first. Not necessary. Just show up and fill out the paperwork. I thought I should at least see where I would be working first, so, in a way, I interviewed them. Who wouldn't want to work for SGI? They were just showing their strength as a big-time player after the huge success of Spielberg's movie. Plus, I loved their workstations. It was an amazing opportunity, and the pay was outrageous. I felt as if my ship had come in.

It was during this period, 1995 through 2004, that SGI acquired a number of different companies and incorporated their technologies into the company. These acquisitions included MIPS, Alias Research and Wavefront Technologies (both merged into Alias/Wavefront), Cray Research, and Intergraph Workstations. Not all of these acquisitions paid off and were eventually sold to other companies. But in the meantime, SGI was riding high on the success of their film work and created a spinoff division called Silicon Studio, the purpose of which was to concentrate on their motion picture technology. From 1995 to 2002, all films nominated for Visual Effects Oscars were created by SGI systems. The technologies were also used in numerous commercials, such as for Apple, Coca-Cola, Budweiser, Dodge, United Airlines, and many more.

Also of importance to SGI during this period was the deal they signed with Nintendo to develop the Reality Coprocessor used in the Nintendo 64 video game console. The deal was signed in 1993 and announced in August of that year. The console itself was released in 1996. There was an incentive given to employees which awarded a free Nintendo 64 if you submitted a resumé for someone who was eventually hired. I got one of those free N64 consoles and I still own it.

During this time period, there were a number of celebrity guests visiting the SGI campus, including Michael Jackson and presidential candidate Bill Clinton. Occasionally, there would be impromptu rock concerts given by famous artists such as Huey Lewis and the News. Their year-end parties were usually held in large prestigious venues, always with famous names for entertainment. One such party I attended, at the San Jose Arena (now called the HP Pavilion) had Natalie Cole as its main attraction. This was just a part of the SGI culture that everyone was proud and excited about. The company fostered a friendly party atmosphere that ultimately may have been part of its undoing. For instance, every Friday SGI hosted what they called the weekly "beer bash". As you might expect, this involved lots of beer in a work atmosphere. Food and entertainment would go along with these weekly events, and it was certainly great for company morale, but there was always the chance that someone might leave this event drunk, and that's never good for a company to encourage drinking and driving. I, myself, tended to skip these events (except occasionally) because I don't like to drive after drinking. Also, as part of this SGI party atmosphere, employees felt they were given permission to keep booze in their workspaces, with many cubicles occupied by mini-fridges full of food and drink, often of an alcoholic nature. What was essentially a firing offence at most companies was tacitly allowed at SGI.

Speaking of cubicles, they were often decorated with exotic furniture and plush comfy chairs and sofas, and many cubicles had Japanese Shoji room dividers for privacy. Stereo sound systems were not uncommon as well, and employees were given permission to play it loud, as long as it didn't annoy too many neighbors. Afterhours interactive role-playing games were encouraged, and many's the time I participated in multi-player Doom or Dungeons and Dragons.

During my time at SGI I witnessed several pranks. Because the SGI Indy workstations came equipped with camera and microphone for tele-conferencing (a first of its kind, as far as I know, and a precursor to today's modern tele-conferencing software such as Skype or Zoom), and also because the SGI campus required all workstations to have free and open superuser access, one of my co-workers played a pretty nice prank on one of the members of our team. Having superuser access allowed anyone to control the speaker output and using the microphone on your own workstation allowed you to actually send audio to another workstation. So, the prankster would periodically whisper the victim's name in a ghost-like fashion. It was hard to tell where the sound was coming from, so it drove the victim crazy trying to figure out if it was real or just the voices in his head.

At SGI it was a tradition to decorate the cube of someone celebrating a birthday, so that the person arriving to work on the day of the birthday would find decorations such as balloons and streamers. Pretty much the typical sort of festive decorations you would expect to find at any birthday party. Well, one day it went a little too far and the person arriving for work found his cubicle completely filled with balloons! It took the better part of the day to deflate and remove all the balloons so that actual work could be done. This was the sort of nonsense happening at startups and established companies during the Dot-Com boom.

But the most elaborate prank I observed was when a co-worker returned from vacation to find his cubicle had been moved. In fact, it had been moved to a stall in the men's public bathroom!

Finally, there was the annual LipSync contest which took place at the Shoreline Amphitheatre, just across the street from the main campus. Anyone familiar with the live performance rock 'n' roll scene will likely recognize this venue for its stellar concerts, such as the annual Neil Young Bridge Concert (now defunct) and shows by everyone from the Eagles to Black Sabbath to Bob Dylan. It was, and still is, a major rock venue, and SGI had exclusive rights to use it for their annual company event.

In 1995, one of the most significant events in SGI's history occurred, and I was fortunate to be there when it happened. Steven Spielberg, Jeffrey Katzenberg and David Geffen formed a new company, DreamWorks SKG (after the initials of its founders) and SGI was the computer company they chose to team up with. From the Los Angeles Times, dated June 1, 1995:

MOUNTAIN VIEW, Calif. —

DreamWorks SKG, the hot new movie studio formed by Steve Spielberg, Jeffrey Katzenberg and David Geffen, announced Wednesday that it will hook up with Silicon Graphics Inc., the equally hot computer graphics outfit, to build what the companies describe as the movie studio of the 21st Century.

The alliance, the latest in a string of marriages between the film and computer industries, will develop digital film production systems that will make it possible to create special effects-laden movies--and especially animated films--better and more cheaply.

Silicon Graphics has worked with Spielberg before: It created the lifelike dinosaurs of Jurassic Park. And the company's 3-D workstations were used for the special effects in "Casper," a film produced by Spielberg's production company, Amblin Entertainment.

"Our ambition is to do things people haven't seen before," said Katzenberg, former chairman of Disney's film operations and now chief executive of DreamWorks. "If we're able to dream it up, we'll be able to deliver it eventually," Spielberg added.

Silicon Graphics and video software firm Cambridge Animation will collaborate on a computer animation production system to be used on a feature-length animation film already in production. The system will be in the hands of DreamWorks animators by September of this year. DreamWorks and Silicon Graphics will share the estimated $50 million in development costs.

DreamWorks said it will market the system, the Digital Animation Dreammachine, to others. "There is nothing we are doing or building that we won't make available to others--and not just in our industry," Katzenberg said.

Cel animation will continue to represent the core of animated films. But the computer technology will enable animators to manipulate the images with more efficiency and a greater variety of options. Animation, one of Katzenberg's specialties at Disney, is expected to be a key asset for DreamWorks. And so is technology: DreamWorks has joined forces with PC software giant Microsoft Corp. on a venture that will create multimedia CD-ROMs.

For Silicon Graphics, the alliance represents the opportunity to sell more of its 3-D workstations. At the moment, it sells about $300 million worth of hardware annually to the entertainment industry.

My own personal remembrance of this event:

On June 1, 1995, the entire campus was called to attend a special all hands meeting. Since not everyone could fit into the indoor hall, most of us stood outside, viewing the meeting on a large telescreen. On the screen was CEO Ed McCracken and COO Tom Jermoluk (fondly known as TJ), along with Steven Spielberg and Jeffrey Katzenberg. Missing was David Geffen, the "G" in SKG. The purpose of the meeting, obviously, was to announce the partnership between the three filmmakers and SGI. It was an exciting time for everyone in attendance. I, myself, did not know this was coming. I hadn't really paid much attention to the corporate comings and goings of SGI, but I was certainly aware of the Hollywood connections. In fact, it's the main reason I was hired.

After a short while, all four came outside to a makeshift stage for a little Q&A. Most of the questions were for Spielberg, naturally, and he was very genial and forthcoming. When asked which film he was most proud of, he mentioned the Oscar winning *Schindler's List*, to great applause. I, myself, wanted to ask him which film was his least favorite or his most regrettable, thinking of *1941*. I didn't ask that, though. I didn't want to be a buzzkill. Katzenberg didn't say much. It was mostly the Steven Spielberg show that day.

So, great things were on the way. Or were they? A few years after the partnership was announced, SGI was unceremoniously dumped in favor of cheaper, often free, alternatives in the form of PCs running Linux – a freely available Unix operating system that provided just as much technology for a fraction of the cost. SGI was undone by its own expensive proprietary innovations which were no longer innovative. This spelled the end of Silicon Studio and many layoffs occurred. By this time, however, I had moved on to another company in yet another "can you start tonight" moment. Startup fever was sweeping the Valley in the late '90s and many of SGI's most talented engineers and technical managers were leaving to start or join new startup ventures. One of these was CyberSource, a pioneering e-commerce company founded in part by ex-SGI employees.

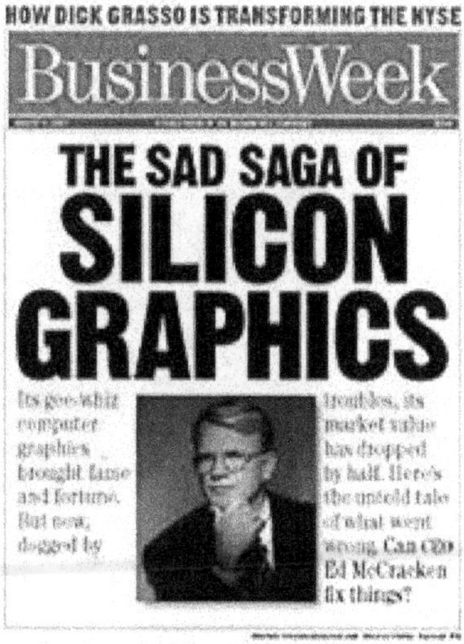

SGI crippled along for a few more years, losing money and market share, and tried and failed to rebrand itself as a supercomputer giant. It was too little too late. On April 1, 2009, SGI filed for Chapter 11 bankruptcy protection and announced that it would sell substantially all of its assets to

Rackable Systems, a deal finalized on May 11, 2009, with Rackable assuming the name Silicon Graphics International. The remains of Silicon Graphics, Inc. became Graphics Properties Holdings, Inc. SGI sold for a mere $25 million. The company was once worth billions, was the darling of Hollywood, and looked to be unbeatable. Now, it would be hard to find anyone who remembers this giant of Silicon Valley. When I wear one of my SGI t-shirts or hats, very few exhibit any sort of recognition. Oh well.

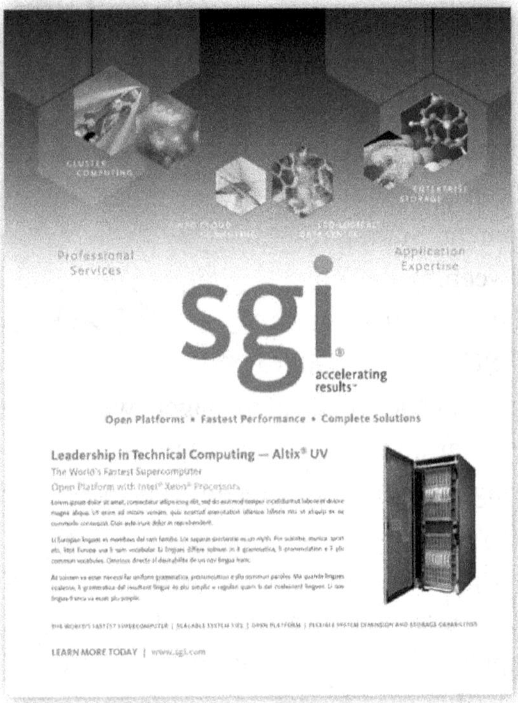

SGI Goes Hollywood

For eight consecutive years (1995–2002), all films nominated for an Academy Award for Distinguished Achievement in Visual Effects were created on Silicon Graphics computer systems. Here is a list of movies made with SGI equipment. This list also includes films where SGI hardware appears on the screen:

The Abyss – 1989
The Hunt for Red October – 1990
Terminator 2 – 1991
Lawnmower Man – 1992
Jurassic Park – 1993
Forest Gump – 1994
The Mask – 1994
The Crow – 1994
Disclosure – 1994
Junior – 1994
Congo – 1995
Jumanji – 1995
Casper – 1995
Toy Story – 1995
Silver – 1995
Frighteners – 1996
Chain Reaction – 1996
First Kid – 1996
Jerry Maguire – 1996

Twister – 1996
Men in Black – 1997
The Peacemaker – 1997
The Relic – 1997
Jurassic Park 2 – 1997
Starship Troopers – 1997
Titanic – 1997
Lost in Space – 1998
Antz – 1998
Sphere – 1998
The Rugrats Movie – 1998
What Dreams May Come – 1998
Star Wars Episode 1 – 1999
The Matrix – 1999
The Mummy – 1999
Scream 3 – 2000
Gladiator – 2000
Hollow Man – 2000
The Adventures of Rocky and Bullwinkle – 2000
The Perfect Storm – 2000
Cats & Dogs – 2001
Evolution – 2001
Final Fantasy – 2001
Lord of the Rings – 2001
Jurassic Park 3 – 2001
Shrek – 2001
Ice Age – 2002

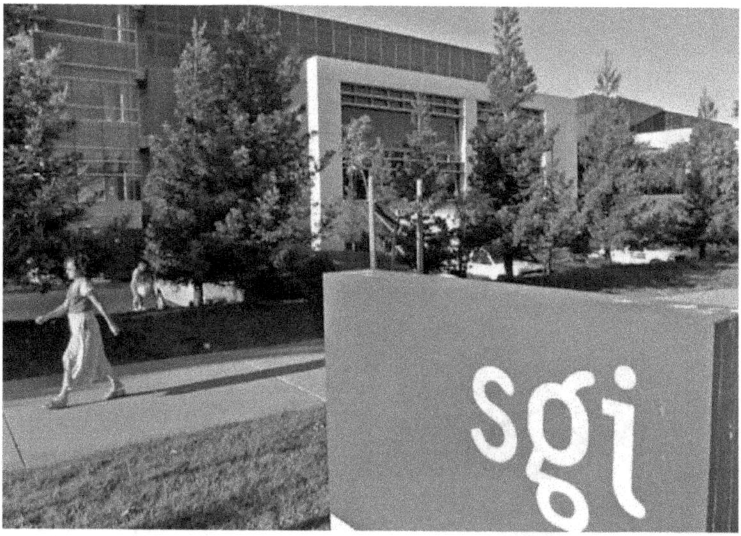

The SGI campus in Mountain View, now occupied by Google

An array of SGI workstations in the 1990s

The Indy – SGI's most popular work-station

The Challenge server

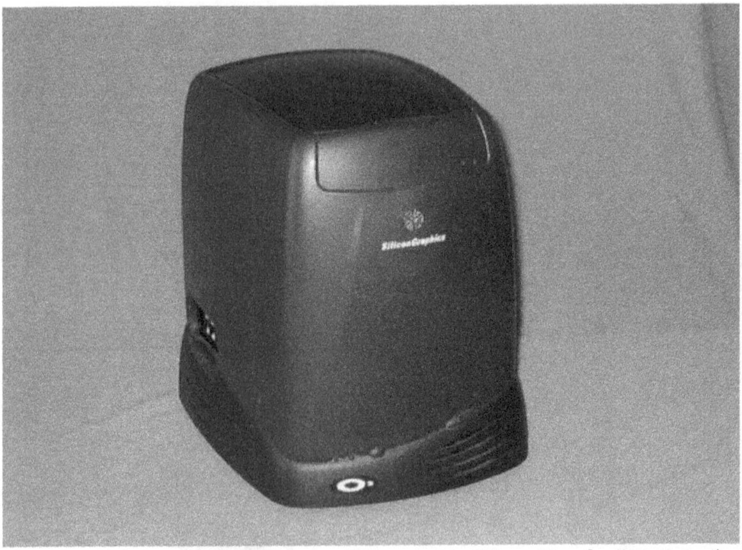

The O2 – SGI's last gasp workstation. When I was still working for SGI, its code-name was "Moosehead".

SGI Computers as Seen in the Movies

SGI laptop (which didn't really exist) as seen in the movie *Congo*

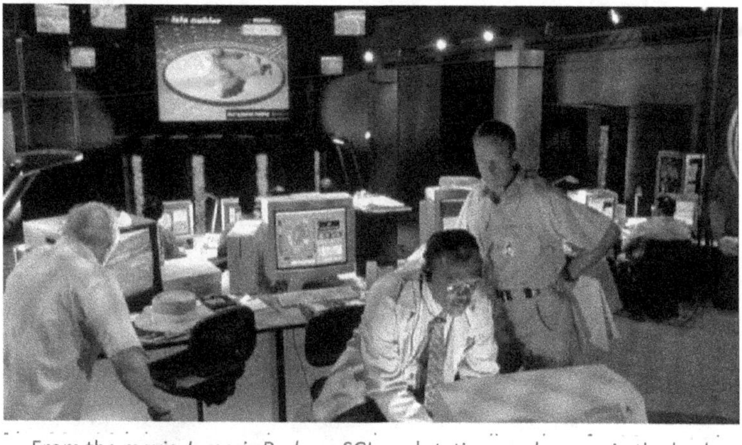

From the movie *Jurassic Park*, an SGI workstation can be seen in the background

An SGI Indy as seen in the 1994 movie *Disclosure*.

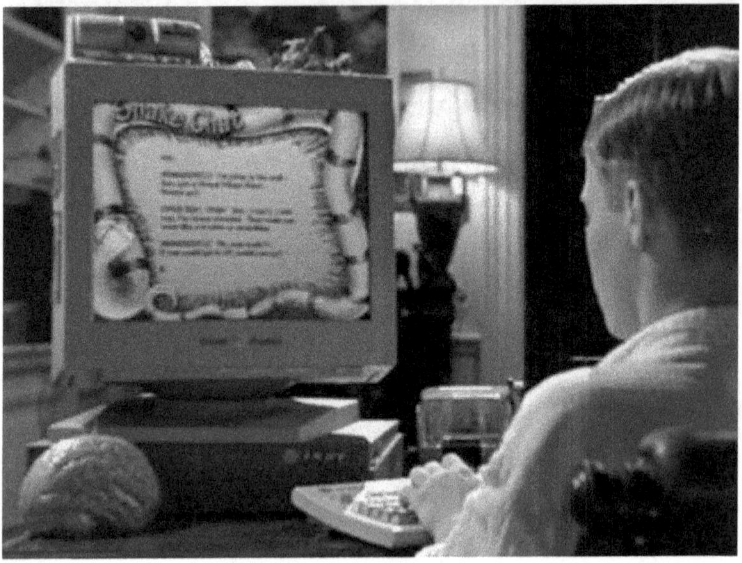

An Indy in the 1996 movie *First Kid*

Tom Cruise sits at his Indy in *Jerry Maguire* (1996)

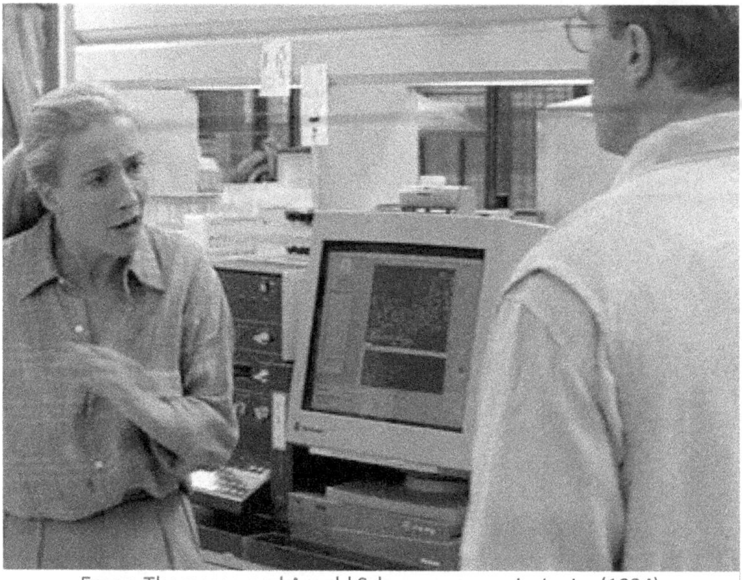

Emma Thompson and Arnold Schwarzenegger in *Junior* (1994)

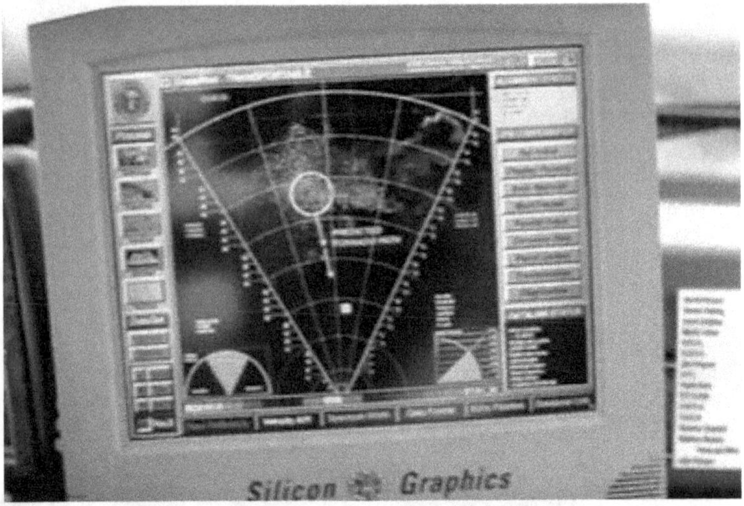

An Indy, as seen in the movie *Twister* (1996)

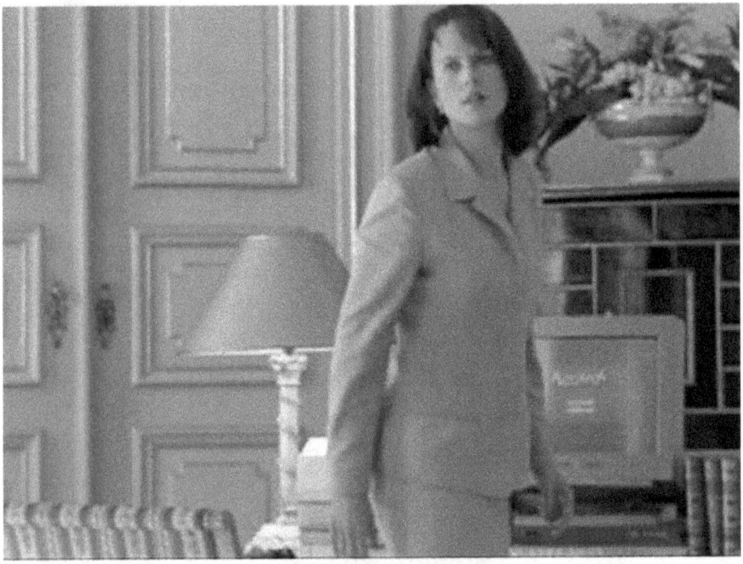

Nicole Kidman in front of an Indy in *The Peacemaker* (1997)

Sun Microsystems

Sun Microsystems was certainly one of the giants of Silicon Valley in the 1980s and 1990s. Sun was originally an acronym for Stanford University Network (again with the Stanford connection) and was founded by Stanford students Andy Bechtolsheim, Vinod Khosla, Scott McNealy, and ultimately Bill Joy, a UC Berkeley computer scientist who helped create Unix BSD. The first CEO was Vinod Khosla and in 1984 Scott McNealy took over as CEO and held that position until 2004.

My first encounter with a Sun workstation was at Ames Research Center in Mountain View when I was primarily involved with running and maintaining the DEC VAX systems that were dominant in the main computer facility at Moffett Field. It was 1982 and Sun Microsystems, which was located in Santa Clara, not too far from Moffett Field, was making its way into the aerospace industry in an effort to compete with SGI and Apollo for dominance in the workstation space. Eventually, Sun would succeed in outlasting both companies and become the de facto workstation company. In fact, for a time, whenever I started working at another tech startup company, Sun was the brand that was most often supplied for my use. However, the original Sun workstation I used at Ames was not very impressive. But over time, Sun proved to be one of the most innovative, and most ubiquitous computer companies during the original heyday of Silicon Valley.

These are some of the important technologies developed by Sun: The Java programming language; the Solaris operating system, based on System V Unix (their first OS was based on BSD Unix and called SunOS); NFS (Network File System); the SPARC architecture. All of these technologies dominated, and still continue to dominate the market. Even though hardly anyone remembers this giant, anyone who has entered the Computer Science field today is likely familiar with Java. Java is an object-oriented versatile language which is the backbone behind the scenes of many modern software applications. It's a portable language used across multiple platforms. Most mobile devices these days use Java.

So, what happened to cause the downfall of Sun? As with SGI, it was the expensive propriety nature of the technology that seemingly doomed it, with PCs and laptops being the much cheaper solution for most companies that used to rely on Sun's expensive workstations. When I was still in the software development business, it was Macintosh laptops or Windows PCs that were the preferred equipment. Much cheaper and more portable. Even Sun's own VirtualBox, allowing the user to install various different operating systems (Windows and Linux) in one single application, made the obsolesce of bulky workstations inevitable. Since VirtualBox runs on various platforms, such as MacOS and Windows, it became a popular virtual environment on which you could run a number of foreign operating systems, including Sun's own Solaris Unix-based operating system. No doubt, it was thought that use of VirtualBox would encourage more people to install Solaris on their laptops, thus increasing the Sun brand. From my own personal experience with VirtualBox, I used it to run Windows and/or Linux on my Mac laptop in various software development jobs which required support for multiple environments. Since you could also run Solaris in VirtualBox, that pretty much eliminated the need to use a Sun workstation. By that time, workstations were pretty much a thing of the past, and workstations were Sun's strong suit.

The technology that Sun innovated still lives today under another brand: Oracle. In April of 2009, Oracle acquired Sun for approximately $5 billion. Compare this to the acquisition of SGI for a mere $25 million. Under Oracle, Sun's products – Java, MySQL database, VirtualBox – are still very popular and indispensable today. Sun may be forgotten, but their legacy lives on.

The Sun founders. Left to right: Vinod Khosla, Bill Joy, Andy Bechtolsheim, Scott McNealy

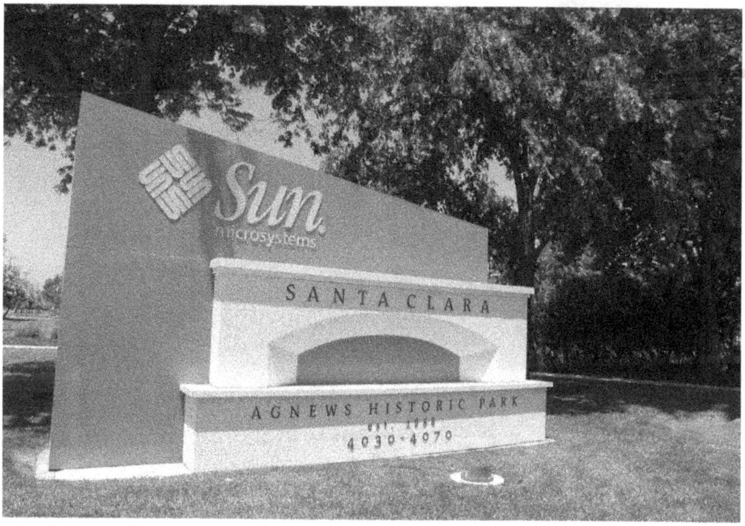

Sun's Santa Clara campus, formerly the site of Agnews Developmental Center.

The Sun 3/60 workstation

The Sun Ultra workstation

The Sun SparcStation – the most popular workstation

The Sun Blade – their entry into the server market

Netscape Communications Corporation

Everyone is familiar with modern web browsers such as Chrome, Internet Explorer, Firefox, Safari etc. But what everyone has likely forgotten is the giant that got the whole thing started: Netscape. It wasn't by any means the first web browser – that distinction goes to NCSA Mosaic – but it was the first mass-acceptance browser that everyone turned to when the World Wide Web broke open the home computer market and drew the ordinary consumer, not just the computer professional or computer science student, to the Internet as we know it.

Founded in Mountain View by SGI founder James Clark along with Marc Andreessen, Netscape Communications Corporation built its browser on the bones of NCSA Mosaic and managed to recruit members of both SGI and NCSA Mosaic to develop the state-of-the-art browser. When I was working at SGI, Netscape was the default browser built into SGI's workstations, and it was told to me that originally Clark wanted Netscape to be an SGI product, but resistance within the company led to his leaving to start Netscape Communications. Whether or not this is true, I can't really confirm, but if true it's just one more mistake that SGI made in its sad trajectory.

Initially called Netscape Navigator, its successor was the Netscape Communicator suite. Netscape Communicator included more groupware features and went beyond a mere browser, as Navigator was.

Things were going great for Netscape until Microsoft's Internet Explorer – offered free with the Windows operating system – kicked it to the ground. Its market share fell from more than 90 percent in the mid '90s to less than 1 percent by 2006. In 1999, the company was purchased by AOL (America Online), but before that, Netscape created the Mozilla Organization and released its source code to encourage further development. Today, Netscape exists in the form of Firefox, which uses the same Gecko engine. AOL stopped supporting Netscape in 2008.

Among the important technologies invented by Netscape are Javascript and SSL (Secure Socket Layer) – both widely used in all modern web browsers. The dynamic content we see in websites today is a direct result of the Javascript language. Prior to that, web pages were static and if you needed to see fresh content, you had to load a new rendition of the page you were looking at, resulting in annoying delays during a page refresh. SSL is what allows security in websites when you are asked to enter sensitive information such as credit card or Social Security numbers. Without SSL, e-commerce would be unthinkable.

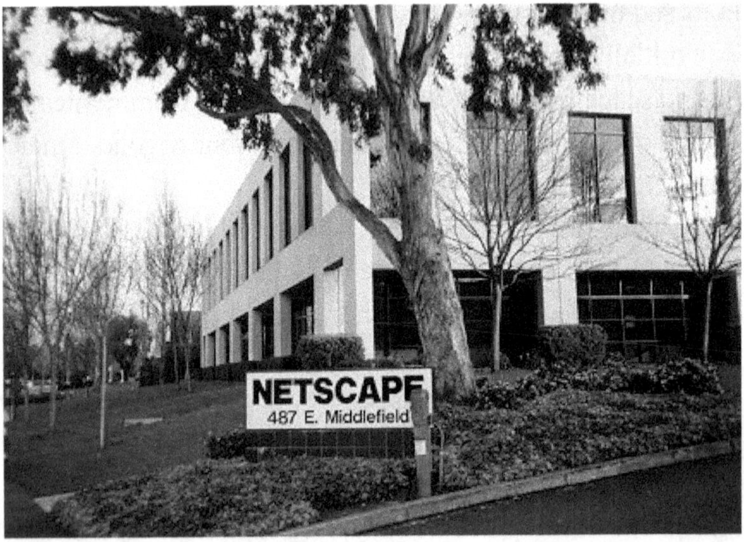

Netscape headquarters in Mountain View

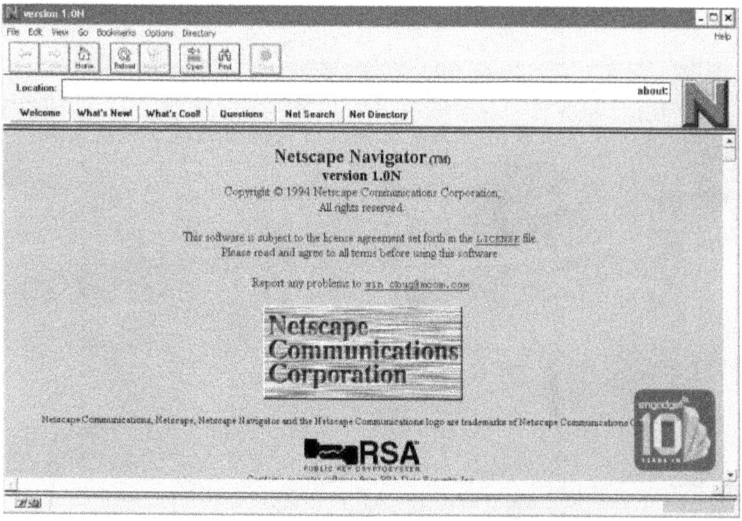

Netscape Navigator version 1.0

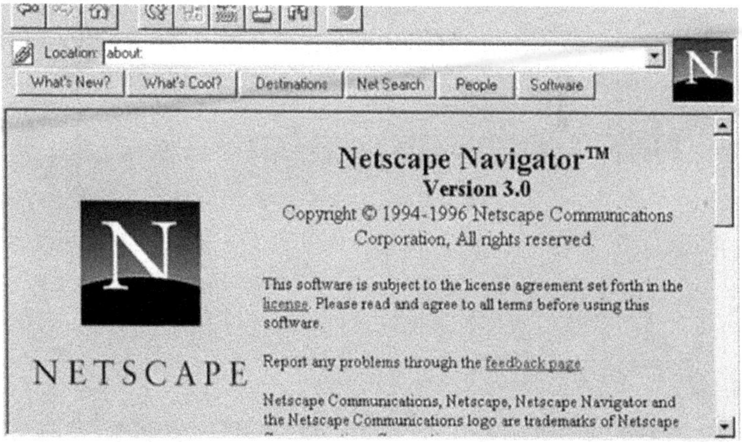

Netscape Navigator version 3.0

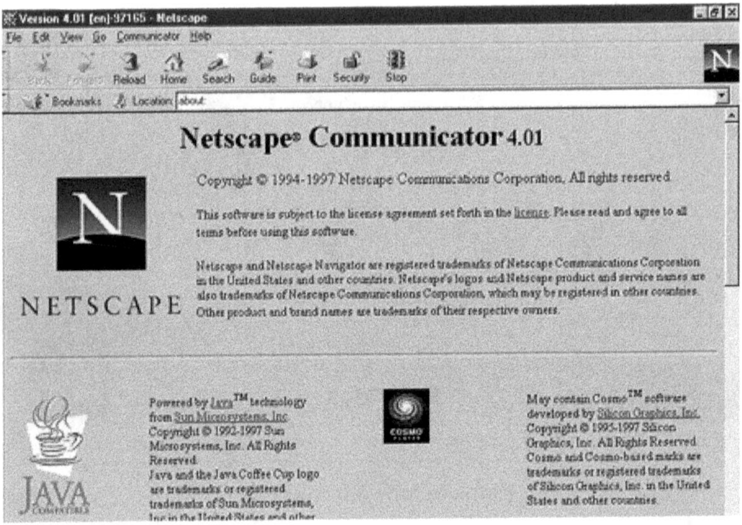

Netscape Communicator version 4.01

Netscape Communicator version 4.5

Netcom

Maybe "giant" is a bit of an exaggeration in this case, but at the beginning of the Internet era, having a reliable Internet Service Provider (ISP) was vital. As previously mentioned, I was involved with setting up the first Nasa-Ames World Wide Web server and used Mosaic and Lynx[10] to surf the web. Since I didn't yet have a home computer, I did all of my personal web surfing at work (sshhh!) but I was interested in getting private e-mail (not through work) and running my own personal web site. Why not? There was no way I was going to use government equipment for this. I needed a commercial private-sector solution. Looking around, I found a number of ISPs that allowed dial-up but no actual web server hosting as such. Some of the ones I did find, such as Prodigy, were too expensive for my taste. I stumbled upon the San Jose ISP Netcom. It was cheap and reliable. Now I had a personal e-mail account and wouldn't have to worry about abusing government equipment. The two would be separated. One problem with Netcom, though, was their lack of HTTP (Hyper Text Transfer Protocol). Without that, you can't really run an effective webserver, but you could, however, use FTP to accomplish the same thing, although in a cruder way.

So, I created the first website for my favorite musical

---

[10] Lynx was a text-based web browser, intended for use on plain non-graphics terminals such as DEC's VT100.

artist: Bob Dylan (a website that still exists to this day). Since Netcom offered dialup shell accounts, I was able to create my HTML (Hyper Text Markup Language) pages using standard Unix text editors (`vi` and `emacs` being the most popular) and also access Usenet using the popular text-only newsreader application `rn` (which was short for "read news"). As I said, Netcom was cheap and reliable. Here's a little history:

The company started in San Jose as a service to students at San Jose State University to access the school from home using dialup. At one time, Netcom served 95% of the San Francisco Bay Area. By the time I had signed up in 1994, the World Wide Web was starting to bloom and as a result, Netcom began to offer their own browser, NetCruiser. The popularity of NetCruiser boosted their profile, and Netcom became one of the top ISPs for its time. I was interested in the company enough to interview for a position there in 1994. I remember the experience well. They were in the top floor of a tall building across the street from the Winchester Mystery House. They occupied several offices in a very ramshackle atmosphere, with boxes stacked up or strewn about, and electronic cables everywhere. They appeared to be a mess. We were just not a good match, but it didn't stop me from using their service until, some years later, I found a better and cheaper solution. By that time, Netcom had disappeared as a brand and other ISPs, such as AOL and Best.com were taking over. Also, new free e-mail services from Yahoo and Google and free web hosting at GeoCities added to the decline of many ISPs. Netcom was one of them. By 2000, all of their shell accounts were terminated and that was pretty much the end of them. Netcom is now completely forgotten except by those who first experienced the Internet through them.

FOR WINDOWS
HOW TO INSTALL:
1) WITH WINDOWS RUNNING, INSERT DISKETTE INTO DRIVE A: OR B:
2) FROM THE PROGRAM MANAGER FILE MENU, CHOOSE RUN...
3) ENTER AISETUP OR BISETUP AS APPROPRIATE. IN THE "WELCOME..." DIALOG BOX, CHOOSE A DIRECTORY FOR INSTALLATION (DEFAULT IS C:\NETCOM)
4) CHOOSE MODEM TYPE, BAUD RATE, AND COM PORT IN THE DIALOG PRESENTED
VERSION 2.1
NETCOM
NETCRUISER™

PRIMA ONLINE
Web Browsing WITH
NETCOM NetCruiser
PAT McGREGOR
GLEE HARRAH CADY

NETCOM
NETCRUISER
Enter the following when prompted:
Registration Code: 03152
Serial Number: 1337124943
(6 month complimentary account)
the complete
internet
access kit
FOR WINDOWS

Chapter 6: The End of the Dream

Much has happened since the 1990s when Santa Clara Valley became the worldwide hub of technological activity that we know it today. When you say "Silicon Valley" today, the immediate thought among most people would be Facebook, Google or Apple. Many people might think of the hit HBO comedy series "Silicon Valley". It could be thought of as a wonderful place where smartphones and social media were created, or the thought might be one of scorn for what that all entails; a complete breakdown of society, perhaps. Or it may be, as in the case of the TV show and various movies, a complete joke. The only thing we know for sure is that it wasn't always that way. There is a lot of hidden history that should be more widely known, and I hope that this book has helped to shed some light on things that were unknown or now forgotten.

As a child raised in the Santa Clara Valley, I was fortunate to have stumbled upon a great career that would have been unthinkable in recent years. Many people, such as myself, were hired for no other reason than the fact that someone was needed to perform tasks that no one had any real first-hand knowledge of, and it was all fresh and new. We were all working our way through things that few people had dreamed of and finding ways to make it all work.

The early history of the valley consisted of many things that have been largely forgotten: the agriculture of the valley that made it the best growing region in the country; the inexpensive real estate that made it attractive to both businesses and suburban families; the importance of Stanford University in establishing the foundation of Silicon Valley technology; the casual and blatant racism that drove the early founders; and the forgotten military and government activity which created the need for information technology in the first place. Unlike many industries, the computer technology which arose from all the scientific activity in the valley was never intended to be used for profit, and yet that's the eventual direction it would take, for better or for worse. Without the space race and without the need for national defense, we would likely not have the things that we now rely upon so extensively. Computers made it all possible, but computers were not always what we imagined them to be.

Silicon Valley today has become overpopulated, overgrown, over-engineered and overblown. It is now very easy for a new or established high-tech company to find staffing merely by contacting any of a dozen different recruiters, each one offering an array of cheap contractors, mostly outsourced from other countries, that really have no interest or actual stake in the success or failure of said company. In the early days, workers at high-tech firms had a great deal to gain or lose, so the interest was very high to produce excellent results. Those results, for the most part, were not money motivated. Sure, high salaries were nice, but in the aerospace and scientific fields no one was looking to become rich. A Nobel prize would be nice, but it wasn't yet about commercial considerations. That would happen once the World Wide Web took hold of everyone's imagination and showed what could be done with personal computers. Still, at the beginning of all of that, it was hard to find people who qualified as experts, so they had to be cultivated. Experts in turn cultivated other experts, and the stakes were high. Innovation was the name of the game, whereas today innovation is for the most part dead. Software Engineers today are all too often asked to regurgitate stale software written by others who simply needed to meet a deadline. Bugs are rampant, and contractors have little impetus to improve anything. It's just a paycheck.

As a former web designer, I am disturbed by the preponderance of JavaScript and the overuse of dynamic web design these days that's geared primarily toward advertisement, not to mention the massive increase in trickery built into web design whereby everyone visiting a web page has the possibility of being misled down destructive paths that were never intended by the original developers of the Internet. Web navigation has become something of chore today, and where at one time the Internet was supposed to be the "Information Superhighway", it has more often than not given way to a twisty maze of paths going nowhere. Still, there are some bright spots. Wikipedia is one of them; a non-profit website that retains the true spirit of the original intention of the Internet. Others, such as Google, continue to provide excellent services sorely needed these days, although they are not completely without their commercial pitfalls.

There is no doubt that today's Silicon Valley is truly standing on the shoulders of giants.

Glossary

AOL – America Online. One of the pioneers in consumer Internet Service Providers. Important features included e-mail and web access.

API – Application Program Interface. The point of entry for users when accessing a computer utility. The API defines the commands and interactions between the user and the computer application.

ARPANET – Advanced Research Projects Agency Network. It was the precursor to what we know today as the Internet.

Batch Job – In the early days of mainframe computers, programs were written on decks of punchcards and submitted through card readers and read into a "batch", which was basically a compiled program.

BBN – Bolt Beranek Newman, also known as BBN Technologies. An American research and development agency located in Cambridge, Massachusetts. They were instrumental in helping to establish the Internet.

CERN – European Organization for Nuclear Research. The acronym doesn't match the description because it's a translation from the original French. The World Wide Web began as a CERN project in 1989.

COBOL – Common Business-Oriented Language. This was the most popular programming language in the early days of IBM mainframes and was used mainly for business applications. It is rarely used or even known of these days.

CompuServe – The first major online service provider of primary importance for sending and receiving e-mail, as well as other methods of cyber communication.

COPS – Computer Oracle and Password System. The first important computer security suite. Written by Dan Farmer in 1989.

CPU – Central Processing Unit. This refers to the heart and soul of the computer. The CPU is what processes instructions that make up programs.

Customer Engineer – Commonly referred to as a CE, this was a hardware engineer hired as an on-site staff member of a computer facility and was on 24 hour standby in case of necessary repairs.

DARPA – Defense Advanced Research Projects Agency. Later just known as ARPA, it was the research and development agency of the US government responsible for creation and development of the Internet.

DCL – Digital Command Language. The proprietary command language used in VAX/VMS.

DEC – Digital Equipment Corporation. A once great giant of the computer industry. Considered at one time to be the number 2 computer company, after IBM. They pretty much invented and marketed the minicomputer.

DECUS – DEC Users' Society. An organization for users of Digital Equipment's popular minicomputers, such as the PDP-11 and the VAX-11/780.

E-commerce – The popular term given to the ability to sell products over the Internet.

E-mail – Uses the SMTP protocol to transfer electronic mail from one computer to the next.

FORTRAN – Formula Translation. A once popular computer language ideal for science and math.

FTP – File Transfer Protocol. The client/server method used to transfer files and documents across the Internet. Part of the Internet Protocol Suite.

Gopher – A protocol designed for sharing documents across the Internet. Ultimately overtaken by the World Wide Web.

GUI – Graphical User Interface. The means whereby the user interacts with a web page or application.

Hacker – This slang term is twofold: In one case it refers to an innovative computer programmer relying on instinct and brute force to develop useful software. In the other case, it refers to a malicious computer user attempting to gain unauthorized access to a remote computer.

HTML – HyperText Markup Language. The language used to create web pages.

HTTP – HyperText Transfer Protocol. The method used to transfer HTML files across the Internet. Belongs to the Internet Protocol Suite.

I/O – Input and Output, i.e. computer code through some manner of submission and the resulting output, either a hardcopy printout or a digital display of some sort.

IBM – International Business Machines. One of the giants and pioneers of the computer industry. Still exists today, although they have long been out of the hardware market and now concentrate on software.

Internet – A global collection of interconnected computer networks using the IP protocol (TCP/IP). Initially comprised of ARPANET, MILNET, and NFSNET.

IP – Internet Protocol. The basis of everything that happens in the Internet. The Internet Protocol Suite contains all of the protocols that all of the network services use to transfer data across the Internet.

IPO – Initial Public Offering. What every startup company and their employees dreamed of. Stock options were a great incentive to join a new company and an IPO was the goal.

IRC – Internet Relay Chat. A client/server application for sending and receiving text messages in real-time. Created by Jarkko Oikarinen in Finland in 1988. Similar to today's text applications on smartphones and tablets.

ISP – Internet Service Provider. A company that allows the consumer to access the Internet and make use of a number of important and popular features of the Internet, such as e-mail and web hosting, among others.

Java – An object-oriented computer language invented by James Gosling of Sun Microsystems. It continues to be one of the most popular languages for backend web design.

JavaScript – Developed by Netscape, this language has nothing to do with the Java language. It is widely used these days to provide the dynamic content you see in most web pages. When used well, it offers a pleasing user experience, but it is often overused to the point of irritation and allows for numerous bugs and potential hacks.

Lynx – A popular and useful World Wide Web client which was designed to run on non-graphical terminals.

MILNET – Military Network. Now part of the Internet, it was originally created as part of ARPANET for the purpose of transferring unclassified Department of Defense documents.

Mosaic – Considered to be the very first web browser. It was developed by NCSA in 1992.

NACA – National Advisory Committee for Aeronautics. The government aeronautical agency that preceded NASA.

NASA – National Aeronautics and Space Administration.

The successor to NACA. A great many of the computer technologies we take for granted today were developed for NASA during the initial space race.

NCSA – National Center for Supercomputer Applications. NCSA developed free application such as Mosaic and the Apache HTTP server for the World Wide Web, as well as the telnet protocol for accessing remote computers in an interactive fashion.

NFS – Network File System. A method, developed by Sun Microsystems, for sharing filesystems across different computers.

NFSNET – National Science Foundation Network. Created in 1985 to promote advanced research and education networking in the US. Since 1995, it has been incorporated into the Internet.

NNTP – Network News Transfer Protocol. Primarily used for Usenet, it is part of the Internet Protocol Suite.

OS – Operating System. An IBM operating system used by the IBM 360.

PDF – Portable Document Format. The most common output format being used these days for text and images. Developed by Adobe in 1993.

PDP – Programmed Data Processor. Developed by Digital Equipment Corporation in 1963. The PDP was the first minicomputer.

Perl – One of the most popular scripting languages. It was, for a while, the backbone of WWW processing. It is still very versatile and widely used.

PHP – Currently the most popular scripting language for the web. It doesn't really stand for anything, but originally it stood for Personal Home Page.

Punchcard – An outdated computer I/O media that was widely used in the early days of mainframe computers for entering data. Each punchcard contained a line of code that could be read by a card reader. It was a primitive method of inputting data before the widespread availability of terminals and graphic devices.

Python – One of the most popular scripting languages currently being used in software development.

RDBMS – Relational Database Management System. A subset of DBMS (Database Management System) specifically designed for relational databases.

SATAN – Security Administrator Tool for Analyzing Networks. An advanced system security suite written by Dan Farmer in 1995 while working for SGI. They subsequently fired him due to a misunderstanding about the nature of the software.

SGI – Silicon Graphics Incorporated. A giant in the workstation market. They were the hardware and software behind the special effects seen in most films in the 1990s and 2000s.

SMTP – Simple Mail Transfer Protocol. The method for sending and receiving e-mail. Part of the Internet Protocol Suite.

Software Engineer – A fancy name for computer programmer.

Spreadsheet – Output in the form of a table or chart.

SSL – Secure Socket Layer. The original protocol establishing authenticated and encrypted links between networked computers. Created by Sun Microsystems.

Sun Microsystems – A major workstation company in the 1990s. Now owned by Oracle.

TCP/IP – Transmission Control Protocol. The main transfer protocol upon which other network services such as FTP and HTTP rely.

TSS – Time Sharing System. An IBM operating system specific to the IBM 360.

UNIX – One of the most popular operating systems currently in use. Developed at Bell Labs in 1969, it was written entirely in the C language and is easily portable to a number of different platforms. The fact that the source code is free allows for easy installation and its popularity allows for a wide level of support among users and engineers.

URL – Uniform Resource Locator. The means by which a website is located and accessed through a web browser.

Usenet – The original social media created in 1980 as a means of connecting large groups of computer professionals and students wishing to engage in technical or recreational discussions. Usenet is still in use today, although it has largely fallen out of favor.

UUCP – Unix-to-Unix Copy. This was an early data transfer model used for the purpose of transferring files from one computer to the next until finally reaching the proper destination.

VAX – Virtual Address eXtention. Developed by Digital Equipment Corporation as a replacement for the PDP series. The first VAX was developed in 1977 and ceased production in 2000.

VisiCalc – The first spreadsheet program for personal computers. It was the Killer App that brought home computers into vogue for the average consumer.

VMS – Virtual Memory System. The VAX operation system. It was a proprietary multi-user multi-processing system very popular during the heyday of Digital Equipment Corporation in the 1980s and 1990s.

WAIS – Wide Area Information Server. A client/server text server now superseded by the World Wide Web.

World Wide Web – Also referred to as WWW, this is the protocol widely used for transferring data across the Internet in an interactive visual fashion. It was the Killer App that brought the Internet to the consumer public at large.

Bibliography

Clyde Arbuckle (1986). Clyde Arbuckle's *History of San Jose*. Smith McKay Printing.

John K. Waters (2002). *John Chambers and the Cisco Way: Navigating Through Volatility*. John Wiley & Sons.

Laws, David (January 7, 2015). "*Who named Silicon Valley?*". Computer History Museum.

Tajnai, Carolyn (May 1985). *"Fred Terman, the Father of Silicon Valley"*. Stanford Computer Forum. Carolyn Terman.

Burlingame, Dwight (August 19, 2004). *Philanthropy in America: A Comprehensive Historical Encyclopedia*. ABC-CLIO.

Tuterow, Norman E. (2004). *The governor: the life and legacy of Leland Stanford, a California colossus, Volume 2*. Arthur H. Clark Co.

Issues in Cyberspace: From Privacy to Piracy. Britannica Educational Publishing. 1 November 2011 Gillmor, C. Stewart. Fred Terman at Stanford: Building a Discipline, a University, and Silicon Valley. Stanford, CA: Stanford UP, 2004.

"William B. Shockley, 79, Creator of Transistor and Theory on Race". New York Times. 14 August 1989.

Michael Riordan & Lillian Hoddeson (1998). *Crystal fire: the invention of the transistor and the birth of the information age.*

Bureau of Yards and Docks, US Navy (1947). *Building the Navy's Bases in World War II; History of the Bureau of Yards and Docks and the Civil Engineer Corps, 1940-1946.* Washington, D.C.: U.S. Government Printing Office.

Hall, Frederic (1871). *The History of San José and Surroundings: With Biographical Sketches of Early Settlers. San Francisco, California:* A.L. Bancroft and Company.

Foote, Horace S. (1888). *Pen Pictures from the Garden of the World, Or Santa Clara County, California. Santa Clara County, California:* Lewis Publishing Company.

Munro-Fraser, J. P. (1881*). History of Santa Clara County, California: Including Its Geography, Geology, Topography, Climatography and Description.* Alley, Bowen, & Company.

Sawyer, Eugene T. (1922). *History of Santa Clara County, California with Biographical Sketches of the Leading Men and Women of the County.* Los Angeles, California: Historic

Record Company.

"Digital Equipment Corporation: Nineteen Fifty-Seven to the Present", DEC Press, 1978.

David Donald Miller (1997). *Open VMS Operating System Concepts.* Elsevier.

Alan R. Earls (2004-06-30). *Digital Equipment Corporation.* Arcadia Publishing.

Edgar H Schein; with P. DeLisi; P. Kampas; M. Sonduck (2003-07-01*). DEC is dead, long live DEC.* Berrett-Koehler Pub.

Jamie Parker Pearson (September 1992). *Digital at work: snapshots from the first thirty-five years.* Digital Press.

Glenn & George Harrar Rifkin; George Harrar (1988). *The Ultimate Entrepreneur: The Story of Ken Olsen and Digital Equipment Corporation* McGraw-Hill/Contemporary.

C. Gordon Bell; J. Craig Mudge; John E. McNamara; Digital Equipment Corporation (1978*). Computer engineering: A DEC view of hardware systems design.*

Bowen, Jonathan (2001). *"Silicon Graphics Inc.". In Rojas, Raúl (ed.).* Encyclopedia of Computers and Computer

History. New York: Fitzroy Dearborn Publishers, The Moschovitis Group.

"Silicon Graphics, Professional IRIS 4D/50GT." Computer History Museum.

"Churchill Club Presents: Scott McNealy in Conversation with Ed Zander" (Press release). Churchill Club. February 24, 2011.

Stephen Shankland (January 27, 2010). *"Oracle buys Sun, becomes hardware company"*. CNET News.

Bechtolsheim, Andreas; Baskett, Forest & Pratt, Vaughan (March 1982). *The Sun Workstation Architecture (PDF) (Technical report).* Stanford University Computer Systems Laboratory.

Lawler, III, Edward E.; Worely, Christopher G. (2011). *"Identity as a Guidepost to Strategy". Management Reset: Organizing for Sustainable Effectiveness.* John Wiley & Sons.

"America Online Inc. Completes Acquisition of Netscape Communications Corp.". Business Wire. March 17, 1999. Retrieved July 1, 2012.

"Netscape Launches Groundbreaking Netscape 6 Browser".

netscape.com. December 13, 2001. Archived from the original on December 13, 2001.

McPherson, Stephanie Sammartino (2009). *Tim Berners-Lee: Inventor of the World Wide Web.* Twenty-First Century Books.

Wagner, Richard Allan. *"The Truth About Sarah Winchester, the Belle of New Haven".*

Ignoffo, Mary Jo. *"Captive of the Labyrinth: Sarah L. Winchester, Heiress to the Rifle Fortune."* Columbia, MO: Univ. of Missouri Press, 2010

Photo Credits

Page 1, 7, 10, 11 – History San Jose Research Library

Page 13 – San Francisco Chronicle

Page 15, 38 (top) – AlamedaInfo.com

Page 22 – AmericanRails.com

Page 26 – Engineering and Technology History Wiki

Page 29 – Stanford News Service

Page 32 – John Howells

Page 34 (top) – San Francisco Chronicle. (bottom) –University of Southern California

Page 35 (top and bottom) – California Images

Page 36 (top and bottom) – WinchesterMysteryHouse.com

Page 37 (top) – Joe Mercier/Shutterstock.com. (bottom) – sanjoseca.gov

Page 38 (bottom), 146 (bottom) – San Jose Mercury News / Eugene H. Louie

Page 41 (top and bottom), 42 (top) - Palo Alto Historical Society.

Page 42 (bottom) – CollegeConsensus.com

Page 43, 56, 116, 120-121, 139 (bottom) 140, 151 (top) – Computer History Museum

Page 44, 49, 51, 55, 61, 69, 70, 71, 72 – IBM Photo Archives

Page 45, 60 (top), 61 (top and bottom) – NASA Photo Archives

Page 50, 54, 66-64, 74-85, 120 (top) – Nancy Hart

Page 64 (bottom) – Telstar Logistics

Page 68 – Charles Babbage Institute

Page 96 (bottom) – Norsar

Page 112 – U.S. National Archives

Page 118 (top) – Boston Globe.

Page 123 (bottom) – Higher Intellect Vintage Wiki

Page 124 – Twentieth Century Fox

Page 140 (top) – Higher Intellect Vintage Wiki

Page 141-144 – Starring the Computer Website

Page 146 – InfoWorld

Page 149 (top) – Kleiner Perkins (bottom)

Page 150 (top) – Robert Harker (bottom) oldcomputer.info

Page 151 (bottom) –Berkeley Software Distribution

Page 154 (bottom) – K W Reinsch

Page 161 – Silicon Angle

All others public domain.

Index

V

W

Y

Acknowledgements

I would like to thank many people for making this book possible, not the least of whom were the hiring managers who took a chance on me in spite of the fact that I had limited experience with computer technology, and in some cases none at all. I would like to thank my good friend Doug Merchant, who recommended me for my very first computer job. Like me, Doug had no experience with computers when he was offered his job, but he certainly proved to be a perfect match for the computer industry, and his recommendation kickstarted my career in a big way. Also, the following were instrumental in helping to build my momentum: Stan Uyeda, Al Wiersma, Fred Silva, Tom Arnold, Pamela Ruhl, Jesse Rendleman, David Schairer, Gretchen Schiffer, Julian Ostrow, Rob Field, Mike Andersen, and many many more. But most of all, I would like to thank my wife, Nancy, for putting up with all my nonsense and encouraging me to finish this book. I could never have done it without her!

John Howells

STATE OF NEW MEXICO
"SPACE AGE RESEARCH CENTER FOR THE FREE WORLD"
"Why we chose the NCR 315 Computer with CRAM."
—STATE OF NEW MEXICO, Santa Fe, New Mexico
NCR PROVIDES TOTAL SYSTEMS—FROM ORIGINAL ENTRY TO FINAL REPORT—
NCR

Other books of interest

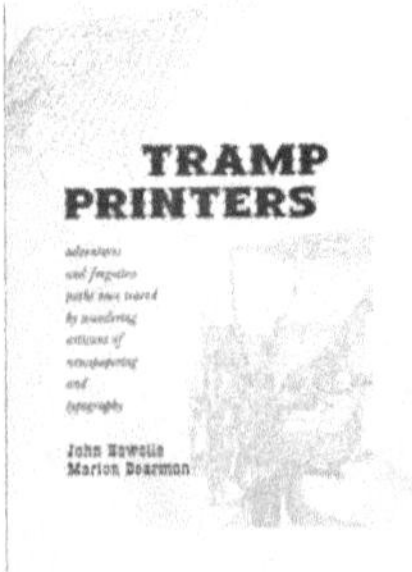

Tramp Printers by John Howells (my Father) and Marion Dearman. Recollections of traveling printers during the "hot metal" era. Beginning with Johannes Gutenberg's invention of movable type in the 15th Century to the end of a 500-year tradition with the beginning of computerized "cold type" in the 20th Century.

Skipping Reels of Rhyme by John Howells. Nominated for the 2019 Association for Recorded Sound Collections Awards for Excellence in Historical Recorded Sound Research. In 1994, the first comprehensive website devoted to the works of Bob Dylan was created. This book presents some of the original articles written for the site, concentrating on the unreleased tapes of Bob Dylan, with commentary on the merits of each tape.

Blown Out on the Trail by John Howells. Nominated for the 2020 Association for Recorded Sound Collections Awards for Excellence in Historical Recorded Sound Research. This is the second in a series of books dealing with the unreleased recordings of Bob Dylan. This edition deals with the two decades from 1976 to 1996, often thought of as his "lost in the wilderness" years. This book is a guide to the best and most worthwhile of the rare and unreleased recordings from those years.

Visit http://tangiblepress.net for more information.